D0900079

PS
3503   Bragdon, Claude
.R238   Fayette
M4
1972   Merely players

DATE DUE

0165 01 204566 01 B   (IC=1)
BRAGDON, CLAUDE FAYE
MERELY PLAYERS
(2) 1972C PS3503.R238M41972 #1

Onondaga Community College
Rte. 173, Onondaga Hill
Syracuse, New York 13215

MERELY PLAYERS

" Travail of the Soul " by Oskar J. W. Hansen.

MERELY PLAYERS

BY

CLAUDE FAYETTE BRAGDON, 1866-1946

"All the world's a stage,
and all the men and women merely players."

—SHAKESPEARE

Essay Index Reprint Series

BOOKS FOR LIBRARIES PRESS
FREEPORT, NEW YORK

The Sidney B. Coulter Library
Onondaga Community College
Rte. 173, Onondaga Hill
Syracuse, New York 13215

Copyright 1905, 1919, 1924, 1928, 1929
by Claude Bragdon.

Reprinted 1972 by arrangement with
Alfred A. Knopf, Inc.

Library of Congress Cataloging in Publication Data
Bragdon, Claude Fayette, 1886-1946.
   Merely players.

   (Essay index reprint series)
   I.   Title.
PS3503.R238M4   1972   814'.5'2   72-5692
ISBN 0-8369-2983-7

PRINTED IN THE UNITED STATES OF AMERICA

Dedicated to

A. S.

For permission to reprint some of the material included in this book thanks are due to *The Architectural Review, The Book Lover, House and Garden, The New York World, The Commonweal, The New York Herald Tribune, The Outlook and Independent,* the *Dial,* Scribner's, *The Star, Arts and Decoration, The Bookman,* and to the *Frederick A. Stokes Company.*

CONTENTS

[ix]

CONTENTS

ILLUSTRATIONS

INTRODUCTION

THIS is the sort of book which I fancy I should like to read if written by one other than myself: no theorizing, little philosophizing, but an account of people known and things seen or experienced — the garnered honey of life's garden. It never occurred to me until lately that I was qualified to write such a book, or that I had the necessary material, for my life has been sedentary and unadventurous. My brother-in-law once dubbed me a cosmopolite of central New York, and although this is too geographically limiting, it is true that save for a *Wanderjahr* in Europe in my youth, I have seldom travelled beyond the confines of the great American Pie Belt. Of late, however, I have come to realize that simply by staying on the same shelf long enough a man comes to assume the sort of importance which attaches to a first edition. The common and unvalued experience shared by many, as these diminish in number with the passing years, becomes unique and precious in the person of the survivor: if we hear said of one man, " He was a slave," or of another, " He knew Lincoln," how suddenly interesting we find them! Although not yet an ancient, I am old enough to invoke this order of interest on the part of the younger generation. Just now they are making pilgrimages to Hoboken to see Boucicault's play, After Dark; to them it is antiquarianism; when I tell them that I saw it when it was fresh as The Front Page, they lend an eager ear. Moreover, everyone seems to be interested in the theatre, whether of yesterday or of today, and as I happen to have had a near view of both, I have drawn upon this experience in *The World of the Theatre*.

A second encouragement to write this kind of a book derives from the fact that although I am neither peripatetic nor gregarious, I happen to have known, and known rather intimately, a number of persons then obscure, who afterwards emerged upon the lighted stage of the world in ways more or less dramatic: I knew Adelaide Crapsey; Willard Straight went to China on my suggestion that the Orient was the place to learn to paint; with Nicholas Bessaraboff I introduced the Russian philosopher Ouspensky to the English speaking world; at one time I saw a great deal of Francis Grierson, an important and romantic figure in American letters; Louis Sullivan, the pioneer of architectural modernism, was a friend of mine. It is to such as these that I devote the second section of my book, *The World of Men*.

For seven years it was my privilege to live in a state of domesticity with a person who seemed to me a reincarnation of a Delphic priestess — that is to say, my wife, Eugenie, was gifted with strange powers of prophecy and divination. Some of her oracular messages I collected and published in a little book called Oracle; but there were many others of a more personal nature, and of an altogether different character, which I withheld. I feel that some of these can now be given out also, and these messages, together with the narratives of how they came to be written, chiefly constitute the final section, *The World of the Wondrous.*

CLAUDE BRAGDON

New York
May, 1929.

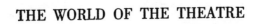

THE WORLD OF THE THEATRE

I

THE STAGE DOOR

IF light, instead of being the effect of chemical or electrical action, were the product of human emotion, brilliant in proportion to the emotional intensity, the light which would emanate from the stage door — a hole in the wall up some dark alley — would far outshine any which now illuminates the theatre entrance on the thronged thoroughfare. I shall indulge in no rhetorical musings on bright dreams and blasted ambitions in this connection, nor recall fond memories of the Famous and the Fair. " Out, out, brief candle! " " *Sic transit gloria!* " — consider these thoughts thought, these sayings said. The only point I wish to make is that the insignificant, shabby, remote and generally unregarded rectangle of the stage door is an aperture through which flows nightly a vari-colored stream of vivid, tumultuous life.

I have often thought that I should like to write a play and call it The Stage Door, though perhaps a more appropriate title in this winter of our discontent would be, All Ye Who Enter Here, Leave Hope Behind. The setting for such a play need be no bigger than the coal bin of a Long Island house, and it would be arranged and furnished something like this:

First of all there would be a chair and desk for the doorman; above the desk would be a list of the dressing rooms and their occupants, and beside it a key-rack and letter box, some of the pigeon-holes empty and others full. Somewhere, in sight and sound of everyone, would be a coin-box telephone, living in a state of indecent exposure for the repository of so many tender and tragic messages — assignations, duns, oaths and veiled obscenities. Indeed, this fateful casket has become the modern abode of the Three Sisters, now metamorphosed into thousands, each wielding a metal plug on the end of a cord in place of the traditional shears: " You'd better come home, your husband's drunk! " — clip! " They took her to the hospital this morning " — clip! " He says you're not the type " — clip! " Darling, are you going to meet me tonight? " — clip, clip!

On the wall would be a bulletin board containing the latest edict of the Actors' Equity; a notice of the next rehearsal, signed by the stage manager; a soiled business card or two, and perhaps a press clipping containing a favorable notice of the show and actors by a friendly critic, but never, by any chance, one adverse. There might be also a calendar, a poster, or even a picture or two, and a rack containing Christian Science literature, but the only other essential properties would be a clock, a water cooler and a cuspidor, though in this particular case, for the furtherance of the stage business, I should introduce a battery of four superannuated orchestra chairs, placed against the up-stage wall. In the right hand transverse wall would be an opening leading to the stage and dressing rooms, with a glimpse of an iron stairway; and in the left hand wall the stage door.

I should have my play begin towards eight o'clock on any winter night, with the doorman discovered. He would be a kind, wise old Irishman, a sort of cross between Saint Peter without whiskers and a bunch of keys, and Charon without an oar, through much drenching in human passions immune at last to Mara's poisoned arrows, a serene and for the most part silent watcher of the fret of the tide through the stage door. Enter, the crew! More affluent than most of the actors, some have driven in from Long Island or from Jersey in their own cars. The parts of the flymen, whose occupation is only a little less sedentary than that of the statue in front of the Cooper Union, would have to be taken by fat men, and of the carpenters and electricians by lean. They would arrive singly and in couples, their hats over their eyes or at a bad angle, dropping their cigarette stubs in the alley before they enter, as the fireman might be about. They would pass through, and after they had set the stage for the first act you may imagine them playing pinocle in the property room or reading the sporting page — for they idolize physical prowess, and if the word is passed around that Tunney or Dempsey is out front, they come as near as a stage hand can come to having stage fright.

The members of the company would trail in after the crew, but by them unregarded, for believe it or not stage hands have for actors a contempt not unlike that of the Labor members of the House of Commons for the House of Lords. But the actors and actresses would exchange pleasant greetings with the doorman and with one another, for as a class they are kindly and warm-hearted in spite of occasional smouldering jealousies and short-lived, secretly nourished hates. They would look for their letters, get their keys from the rack, and be off to their dressing rooms. Meantime, the members of the orchestra, each with his instrument box, will have been arriving, also the wardrobe mistress and her assistant, and last of all the star or staress, who will have dashed up late in a taxi, or in his or her or somebody else's automobile.

Then would supervene an interval of emptiness and silence, which I should of course have to fill up by introducing some modern equivalent of the scene between the butler and the maid with which the authors of yesteryear used to inform the audience about the characters and the plot. An off-stage voice would be heard to shout " Fifteen minutes! " and there would be the distant tuning of instruments, followed by music, faintly audible. Through the opening one would see actors and actresses in costume and grease paint throng into the corridor and down the stair; then would come another off-stage cry of " Curtain! " and the perform-ance — the play within a play — would have begun.

Beyond this point I am vague about my opus, not because I lack characters and a plot, but because there are so many of both I find it impossible to choose; for in every make-believe play — every play given in a theatre — there are at least as many real dramas as there are actors, each one the protagonist of his particular tragi-comedy. The same thing is true, of course, of every person in the audience, but with this difference, that in the case of the actor the dramatis personæ of both plays — his own, of which he is the hero, and that other, in which he is perhaps only a walk-on — are to a certain extent the same, so that one does not interrupt the other (as happens when you and I go to the theatre) but both go simultaneously on.

The only character in my play of whom I am at all sure is the doorman. By reason of his being guardian of the door he'd have to appear in practically every scene, but never obtrusively — a sort of silent watcher, or guardian angel from some other sphere. Eddie Foy, shortly before he died, did a vaudeville sketch in which he took the part of an old stage doorman. My man would be something like that, but less garrulous, with the tolerance and understanding which comes from a long experience of living, and the compassion which comes from an educated heart. The reason I am so sure of this character is because I knew him. Once, at an over-long rehearsal, one of the young women in the company fainted. Much concerned, I carried her into the shabby back-stage vestibule presided over by this man, and asked him to call a cab. The girl revived presently and was taken home by a friend. When they were gone he saw that I was still anxious about her. " I wouldn't worry," he said, "if I were you sir. I think she'll be all right tomorrow — you understand — I've known so many of these girls: I'm old, they tell me all their little troubles; why there was once, sir, when I was remembering more than forty of them in my prayers. They'd write their names down on a piece of paper and say, ' Now pray for me, Jerry, the next time you go to mass,' — and I always did pray for them too. Mary pity women! They have a harder time, sir, than the men."

Though I don't know what my play would be all about, I know, in a way, exactly what it would be like. It would all take place in the stage door vestibule, for that is the only substitute for the green room; small as it is, it is bigger and airier than the dressing rooms, and more convenient to the stage. Everybody flocks there in their odd moments, for gossip, for rough-housing and wise-cracking, for juxtapositions and the smoking of surreptitious cigarettes. The vestibule and the stage are reciprocals of one another, for during ensembles the vestibule would be empty, and when the stage was more or less empty, the vestibule would be filled. But however difficult it might be to arrange it, the action would have to take place in that one spot, for I should want the stage door always in sight. It would come to have a symbolical value: The Gateway of Birth and Death — the birth and death of so many hopes and dreams.

Everything would happen at the end of my play just as I have so often seen it happen, and if you want to know how that is, I refer you to the end of the first act of Debureau, for what Guitry makes to happen in the Théâtre des Funambules in Paris in that far-off time is about what happens in every theatre on Broadway every night — the chatter about the " house " and the " business," the interviews, the appointments, the last goodnights. It's just another example of the timelessness of the temporal — the " eternal return."

The actors would be leaving singly, in groups, in pairs, as soon as they had finished their parts, changed, and scrubbed off their grease paint; though sometimes, if they were in a hurry, they wouldn't wait for this last. For some there would be friends waiting, but one would wait for somebody who never came. Anyway, there would be meetings and greetings of every shade of loving, liking, or disliking. Oh I've seen, and I know how a woman acts when Cupid is in earnest: she wants to touch the beloved one with her hands — straightening his necktie, pinning a flower on his coat, or brushing imaginary somethings off his vest. Always she shines on him the full moon of her face and not the crescent, looking into his eyes with both her eyes. And here's a strange thing: every woman's eyes have the same expression — the Eternal Woman, on her eternal quest for a love which is eternal, looks for a moment out of the windows of some particular woman's eyes.

After the dying down of the applause which signalizes the final curtain, the last-act people would hurry to their dressing rooms. The friends of the star who had been in the audience would crowd the narrow corridor outside the star's dressing room door. Also among them would perhaps be a pressman, a photographer, an autograph hound, the head of a girls' school, all with eyes a-glitter — the glitter of the axe each had come to grind. Meantime, slam, slam, slam goes the stage door. Exit, exit, exeunt, exeunt omnes — a gradual minoration, like the running down of a clock until it stops. All have gone, even the doorman, some on foot, some by subway, some by taxi, some even, smothered in furs, in glittering, be-chauffeured, high-powered, high-priced cars. All are resuming, with a different cast, the play of their personal lives, each in a different setting — a room with a view, a room without a view, a speakeasy, a night club, the Plaza, Pierre's — according to each one's fate or fancy, as the soul wills or has willed in some past life.

Have you ever lingered in a theatre after everyone had left it, with the doors locked and all the lights out save for the stab in the eye of one bare lamp which served only to make the darkness visible? It is a passing strange experience! You feel like the burned-out cinder of some star lost in the gulf of space; above you and about you stretches the primordial void, the abyss. You are rescued from terror by the clatter of the Elevated, a welcome sound for the first time in your life. You feel your way into the stage door vestibule, and are ushered out by the friendly night watchman into the never silent, never unpeopled street. The passing traffic streaks the darkness with fiery pencils. On the cyclorama of the sky the brightness of Broadway is reflected, snuffing out all the stars but one. Would it be Venus or Saturn, do you think?

II

ONE NIGHT STAND

EVEN in the far-off days of my adolescence the town I lived in was already a minor metropolis, inspiring a fierce and jealous civic pride in the hearts of its citizenry, though some anonymous actor, in lyric mood, recorded on the much bescribbled wall of the star's dressing room in the local opera house the following minority report:

> A hick little one-night town,
> A stick little one-night town,
> Uncle Tom, Tan-Joey, burnt cork and banjoey
> Make-me-sick little one-night town.

The opera house was entered from an alley behind the Arcade, a glazed and galleried court, answering the purpose of a local Forum Romanum, since it contained the Post Office and stores. The steps which led from the sidewalk to the auditorium were high and steep as Dante found Verona's, for underneath was one of those saloons with a mahogany bar, beveled plate mirrors and brass foot-rail so dear to the heart of the Old Soak. Here, between the acts and after the performance, the Bench-

[12]

leys, Brouns and Woollcotts of the day and place would give the play and actors thumbs up or thumbs down, making patterns, meanwhile, in the yellow sawdust which covered the floor, with the overflow from their beer glasses and salivary glands.

The interior of the opera house was decorated in a Corinthian style unknown, happily, in Corinth. There was an orchestra circle, a dress circle and a gallery, the latter upheld by slender iron columns which bisected, from the rearward seats, the view of the stage. Mirrors, set at intervals, adorned the walls; downstairs the seats were of ornamental iron, upholstered in green velvet, but in the gallery there were only wooden benches, hard and bare. On either side of the stage were enormous proscenium boxes, always empty except on state occasions — college commencements, charity balls, meetings for the relief of the Kansas Sufferers, and affairs of that sort. These boxes were flanked by fluted columns whose florid capitals sustained broken pediments in the center of each of which was a golden lyre. The studied and self-conscious folds of the purple velvet lambrequins and curtains of the boxes were held in position by gold cords the size of hawsers, and from them depended the archetypes of those great tassels which persist, in painted form, even on the drop curtains of today.

The place was illuminated by means of a gas chandelier consisting of a ring of burners lighted by a taper attached to the end of a long elastic pole, like a fishing rod. The gas footlights were lighted just before the rising of the curtain by a functionary whose appearance was the signal for cries, stampings, whistles and remarks derisive, ribald, personal and derogatory which had the effect of making him hurry through his abhorred task and scuttle quickly behind the curtain like a rabbit frightened by the hunter's gun. There was always some odor of escaping gas about the place, so that even today that odor, by reason of its association with so much of pleasurable excitement, is a voluptuous sensation, affecting me like the smell of lead soldiers, or as the taste, in later life, of the Noah's ark camel affected Oscar Wilde. Sometimes this gas smell became almost lethal, particularly on one occasion which I remember when the violence of the off-stage explosion of the timed infernal machine, placed by the villain of the piece in the hold of the vessel bearing the escaping hero, put out half the lights in the chandelier. In order to allay the anxiety — if any — on the part of the reader as to the fate of the hero, I would say that the next scene discovered him in a waste of artificially agitated waters, on a raft made on the principle of a seesaw, which he kept going with his feet, while with his hands he waved wildly in the direction of a little cardboard steamer being hitched along the top of the water-row by a concealed stage hand.

Clear as is my memory concerning other details, I cannot remember what was painted on the drop-curtain. It was probably a view of the lake of Como with picturesquely disposed contadini in the foreground and a ruined temple somewhere about, all done in dirty umbers and vermilions with the water painted a chalky blue — for this was the canonical thing in those days, as street scenes with advertising inserts became later, and as cloth drapery is today. Travelling companies seldom carried their own scenery in those days, but made the best use they were able of whatever the local house could furnish forth. The equipment, in this case, consisted of the following items: (1) A street scene, in one-point perspective. (2) A forest scene, with wood-wings, ground rows, and foliage borders, all painted in arsenical greens and sepia browns. (3) A kitchen scene, with patches of plaster fallen from the walls, showing the lath. (4) A prison scene, containing a heavily barred, high-up window, and realistically painted chains, heavy enough to sink a ship. (5) A palace scene done in white and gold, with panels of imitation pink silk brocade. These were supplemented with a nondescript interior which could be made to answer equally for Armand's apartment in Paris, or for the Vanastorbilt's reception room on Stuymercy Square. The rooms had no side walls, but only " wings " from between which the actors entered and exited. The flats forming the rear wall ran on grooves and were pushed into position from either side and joined together in the center. When this junction failed to come off effectively one heard curses " not loud but deep," and caught glimpses of agitated hands.

[15]

The furniture and properties were quite as standard-ized as was the scenery, and became as utterly familiar — came, indeed, to possess a certain symbolic value. The gold-framed upholstered sofa and two chairs with "French legs" usually indicated Parisian luxury pur-chased at the price of virtue, and by a similar parity of reasoning the bare deal table and kitchen chair spelled honest poverty. A cherry-red table from the local furni-ture store made its appearance when the action of the play required the entrance of "Annette with lights," or of James, bearing either a tea service (feminine), or a decantur and glasses (masculine). A pink-shaded piano lamp was used on those occasions when the lead-ing lady beguiled with song the time of waiting for her lover, and when she, seated, and he bending fondly above her, enacted the don't-you-remember scene in the last act. Carpets were used only by people of the highest *ton*. There was but one, a parallelogram of bordered brussels, once red, with a distinguishable pattern, but dirt and wear had turned it to a mottled brown. In Camille, I happen to remember, it covered the floor of four several apartments in Paris and its environs at one and the same time. We of the audience accepted these conventions quite uncritically; the play was for us in-deed "the thing" and the things, no matter how gro-tesquely inappropriate, underwent some sort of mystical transubstantiation. Inconsistencies never disturbed us therefore, not even when Camille declared that she

[16]

could pay her debts, amounting to sixty thousand francs, from the sale of her furniture — said furniture consisting of the aforesaid carpet, table, sofa and chairs and a few "throws" and "drapes" and frilled-edged sofa-pillows.

My earliest recollections centering about this cathedral of pleasure are of itinerant Humpty Dumpty and Negro Minstrel shows, forms of entertainment once popular, but now no more. The first consisted of some shabby variant of the conventional English pantomime or harlequinade, but it provided an admirable vehicle for the acrobatic, pantomimic clown, and of Fox, Adams, Miaco my schoolboy friends and I became the sedulous apes. Every Saturday we repaired to a shed full of sawdust on the canal bank and practiced splits, flips, cartwheels and somersaults with such assiduity and success that our prowess became a legend in Number Twelve long after we had left it. When he could escape the teacher's eyes, Tommy used to walk down the school aisle on his hands, at the change of classes; Art could turn a back handspring even with nonchalance; needless to say, these were heights to which I never attained. In later life Tommy became a barkeep'. With slicked hair, parted in the middle, and wearing a white apron, he polished glasses with a napkin, addressing each customer with the same formula, "And what is yours, Mr. A-a-a?" Art, true to his name, followed the primrose path, for he became a member of the

Comedy Four, playing stick towns throughout the West.

The Minstrel Show provoked an altogether different order of psychic reaction in our youthful breasts. The parade of the plug-hatted, linen-dustered company of mummers down the main street, in the wake of the banners and the band, injected into the air of the place an indefinable element of superurbanity and sophistication, which attained its maximum in the evening when the curtain was upfurled upon the serried hemicycle of glittering instruments, gay costumes and black faces, and the interlocutor, with the manners and bearing of Prince Florizel of Bohemia, uttered the awaited words, " Gentlemen, be seated! " the canonical formula with which the elaborate ritual of the First Part always began.

We loved the obvious, carefully led-up-to humors of Mr. Bones and Mr. Tambo, in lesser degree we enjoyed the falsetto singing of When the Robins Nest Again and Only a Pansy Blossom to the ump-pa-pa, ump-pa-pa of the band, but the idol of our particular worship was the banjo soloist who made his appearance in the Second Part, or Olio. He was always dressed in some exaggerated and grotesque costume, his flat shoes were twice the length of his feet, his collar was enormous, with wings which stuck out each side of his black face upon which the vermilion mouth encroached so much that when it was open there was little else to be seen. In one

hand he carried an old fashioned fretless, five-stringed
banjo, and by the other he dragged a kitchen chair.
Arrived (in " one ") at the center of the stage, he would
sit down, cross his legs, wag his free foot a few times,
and after doing a little preliminary wisecracking while
he tuned his instrument, to our ecstatic delight he would
break into some such song as this:

> Oh she was a funny old guy,
> She had a double-barrelled squint in her eye,
> She had an upper lip like the rudder of a ship,
> And a mouth like a crack in a pie.

— or some other equally ribald ditty, my particular
favorite being Get Thee Gone, Girl, Get Thee Gone, Girl,
But the Girl Wouldn't Get Thee Gone.

The repercussions of the Minstrel Show upon our
young enthusiasm drove us to learning the banjo and
the bones, and Tommy became so expert with the tam-
bourine that (having broken many of his mother's plates
in the process of learning) he used to come down the
school aisle spinning his arithmetic on the finger of one
hand and his geography on the other. These flames were
also fed by a third order of entertainment, the Variety
Show, where we fell beneath the spell of such acts as
The Happy Hottentots, Silence and Fun, and wherein
The Spanish Students were the then current equivalent
of the jazz band of today. Dressed in the picturesque
costume of sunny Spain they used to play Secret Love
and The Turkish Patrol March on mandolins and guitars.

It will be noted that these favored forms of entertainment contained little or nothing of sex appeal, so
called. This may have been partly because we were so
young and inexperienced, but it was also partly due to
the fact that sex was a note far less insistently sounded
then than it is now — it was what Mrs. Wharton calls the
Age of Innocence. There were times and occasions,
however, when the sex mystery forced itself upon our
young attention, rather to our bewilderment, it must be
confessed, for what could we be expected to know about
a woman's "honor" or a woman's "shame"? We
missed the point, for example, of such a situation as the
following, which occurred in some Western melodrama
of which I have forgotten even the name.

The action takes place in a mining camp, and the
scene shows the outside of the shack inhabited by the
hero. He loves, and is loved by the mine owner's
daughter. This heroine is seen, by the villain of the
piece, as she is entering the hut alone — unchaperoned.
This in itself, in the then-current moral code is an
utterly damning fact. The miners, aroused and informed
by the villain, gather about the cabin in a lynching
mood. The situation is a tense one: how will the honor
of the girl be saved or vindicated, and how will the hero
escape the fury of the mob? The suspense is relieved by
the door being flung suddenly open, and the hero appears leading by the hand a knock-kneed, broad hipped,
undersized youth, closely resembling the leading lady,

the masses of his curly blond hair tucked underneath the brim of his sombrero. " Meet little brother Phil, from Colorado! " It is thus that virtue triumphs, and the curtain descends amid tumultuous applause.

Here, " where the brook and river meet," I shall end these random recollections of a comparatively unrecorded phase of our theatrical history.

III

CLOWNS AND CLOWNING

SEATED in the New York Hippodrome the other afternoon, watching Toto, the last of its illustrious line of clowns, searching through all his clothes for his other leg and finally feeling for it in his inside pocket, I was convinced anew that the simon-pure clown belonged to a race apart — that like albinos and four-leafed clovers they were altogether extraordinary and exceptional, related less to our common humanity than to one another, no matter how widely separated in time and space. By clown I do not mean the mere funny man, nor the actor who has adopted the clown technique without the clown psychology; I refer only to the true pantomimists, who are able to look at life upside down as it were, and by means of their art and an inevitable rhythm, are able to impose this vision upon others. These are so rare that never more than a few incarnate in any given generation, and their very names — Debureau, Grimaldi, Chaplin — become symbols of a certain *something* to which the sophisticate and the child equally respond: something which we all recognize, and which I shall

[22]

endeavor to analyze — A Philosopher Looks at Clowning might have been a better title for this talk.

Because they alone appear to possess the secret of clown humor, the great clowns are forced, as a rule, to originate their own business, and devise their own scenarios. Their natural language is not speech, but movement, and of that language *things* are the nouns, and *actions* are the verbs. Give Humpty Dumpty his red-hot poker, or his string of sausages on a leash, and he is eloquent and entertaining, but strip him of such accessories — real or imaginary — and we suddenly realize that he is dumb.

The secret of clown humor dwells in its preposterousness, which, it is perhaps necessary to remind the reader, means upside down. The clown does everything differently from the way we would do it, but accomplishes the same result: he walks on his hands, puts his head in his hat instead of his hat on his head, smokes his cigar with the lighted end in his mouth, buttons his coat with a coupling-pin and plays the violin with his cane; if Chaplin is playing the part of a soldier in the trenches who can't get the cork out of a bottle, he holds it up for the neck to be broken by an enemy sharpshooter — and so on. The preposterousness of clown humor is so consistent with itself, and its unreason is so extreme, that it returns, full circle, to perfect reasonableness. When Chaplin, in The Gold Rush, suffering the last extremities of starvation, cooks his shoe in the oven in default of a Thanksgiving turkey, bastes it, carves it, serves it, winds the laces on his fork like spaghetti, and picks the nails out of his mouth as though they were bones, it fills us with unreasoning delight, for having accepted the major premise these corollaries follow as a matter of course.

Clown humor has a curious kinship with the psychology of dreams, for in dreams we are always escaping from preposterous situations in preposterous ways. Du Maurier, in a series of Punch pictures, recounts a typical nightmare which well illustrates this constant characteristic of dreams. He is summoned from his bed and hurried through the streets of London to Albert Hall in a hansom, where he finds that he is expected to sing Sullivan's Lost Chord to a gathered and expectant throng. He discovers, to his consternation, that he has forgotten the air, but Sir Arthur, who is present behind the scenes, obligingly whistles it for him just before he is called. Thus sustained and reassured he steps upon the stage in front of a vast audience only to realize that he is in his nightshirt to escape the ignominy of which he crawls under the grand piano — and so on. This is not only typical nightmare, but it is typical clown humor: the sequences, the surprises, the alternations of satisfaction and despair are such as a good pantomimic clown would revel in.

The psychology of drunkenness is not dissimilar to that of dreams, because inebriation becomes, at a certain point, a waking dream. The only thing which makes the actions of a drunkard funny is that for the time being they spring from the same inverted rationality which pertains to dreams, and is the *sine qua non* of clown humor. The following example establishes this connection very well: I was once riding in the same street car as a drunken man; he had just purchased a new pair of shoes, and was taking them home wrapped up in a paper bag; it occurred to him then and there to put them on, so he took off one of his old shoes and threw it out of the car window, only to find that the new one was so small he couldn't squeeze his foot into it, whereupon he threw that out of the window too, and proceeded to encase his foot in the paper bag, tying it about the ankle with a piece of string, all with the clown's deep seriousness and obliviousness. Everyone in the car, including myself, followed these preposterous, but dream-logical proceedings with the same kind and degree of amusement as did the audience at the Hippodrome when Toto disrobes and hurls his garments one by one into the air, and then, suddenly realizing his exposure, places a small, transparent screen in front of his shins. The sequence and the psychology are identical in both cases.

These and similar parallels between clowning, dreaming, and the somnambulism of the drunkard may serve to explain why the clown is so universal in his appeal: he is the dramatizer of a subjective state or level of psychic life which is itself universal, and of which everyone has had experience. " All the world loves a lover " because we are all — potentially at least — lovers, and all the world loves a clown because in one department of our manifold nature we are all clowns. But there is another and an altogether different reason.

Acrobatics and juggling have always been recognized as part of the technique of clowning. All of the great clowns have possessed this order of adroitness in greater or less degree. Now to become an acrobat and a juggler involves a mastery of rhythm and a power and universality of bodily control far beyond that required of the dancer. The acrobatic art is, in a sense, a higher power of dancing, it is the greater which includes the less, being governed by a higher mathematic, as it were. The acrobat weaves patterns in space of which the dancer is incapable, and to do this submits himself to a training and discipline far more arduous. Charles and Ernest Clarke, the aerialists, practiced their " two somersaults and a twister " at least ten times a day for over a year before ever their hands came together (and every try meant a drop in the net), and it took three and one half years more of practice before they felt themselves justified in exhibiting the feat. This anecdote may seem irrelevant because it has to do with the higher reaches of acrobatics, but the point which I wish to make is that the pantomimic clown, with his acrobatic training, is usually if not a finer, at least a more technically proficient artist than the dancer, and that from this order of proficiency we derive a deep, peculiar and unanalyzable pleasure. This pleasure is certainly akin to that which music itself inspires: in the good old circus days when the motley company of acrobats and clowns used to take turns doing somersaults over the elephants I am sure that I, who am not musical, experienced a pleasure not unlike to that of a musician at an orchestral concert. Both things are mathematical: acrobatics are mathematics made visible — expressed in terms of space; music is mathematics made audible — in terms of time. Quite aside, then, from the humor of clowning, we derive subjective satisfaction from the mathematics — expressed in rhythm — of that order of bodily movement which is the fine fruit of acrobatic training, the preëminent possession of the pantomimic clown, as distinguished from the actor-pantomimist.

The great clowns have always been distinguished by their ability to move their audiences to tears as well as to laughter, and to both at the same time. My first experience of this strange double emotion was provoked by some forgotten episode in the performance of George K. Fox, " the American Grimaldi," in Humpty Dumpty, witnessed as a boy. By his possession of this dual power Chaplin proves himself to be of the superior hierarchy. The clown-image, as it exists in the popular mind is thus paradoxical, for the clown whose heart is not secretly sad underneath his motley is, to that mind, by so much less a clown. The public demands that its supreme symbol of irresponsible human joy shall be equally a symbol of human suffering, as is proven by such plays as Pagliacci, Debureau, He Who Gets Slapped, and Laugh, Clown, Laugh, all based upon the clown-with-a-breaking-heart theme.

It would seem, as a matter of fact, that there is something intrinsically tragic in being, as it were, a priest of pleasure: the clown appears to share this doom no less surely than the courtesan, for the reason that in addition to those " slings and arrows of outrageous fortune " which, just because a clown is a human being, inevitably reach their mark, there are poisoned darts reserved for him alone. To grow old, to grow stiff, to grow feeble, must have for him a poignancy unknown to others, because youth, strength, nimbleness, are the very tools of his trade. No class is more cruel, fickle, forgetful, than the seekers after mere entertainment and pleasure; this may be known theoretically by everyone, but it becomes bitter experience to prize-fighters, ballplayers and clowns who survive their period of highest efficiency and outlast their welcome, so certain it is that if they overstay their moment " hatred's swift repulsions play." This is the theme of one of the most effective scenes in Debureau.

I do not know why it should be so, but there is often some dreadful, macabre element in the way in which clowns' lives end. Three instances of this occur to me: the first great American clown died from the effects of poison in the whitening he used on his face, for he lived before the days of grease paint; a no less famous successor, the children's idol, died alone, unheeded, neglected, in poverty and by his own hand, almost under the shadow of the place of his former popularity, and a third well-known clown, confined to an insane asylum, and denied all means of self-destruction, turned half-back somersaults against an iron steam radiator until he succeeded in fracturing his skull, committing suicide in this strange way.

In the jargon of modern psychology the clown is, in the last analysis, the embodiment and dramatization — burlesqued if you will — of the introvert, the lonely soul, the John o' Dreams. Toto looking for his lost leg in his inside pocket is the symbol of this order of introspection, and the final episode of The Circus is utterly in character with this view of clown psychology. We see the insignificant and forlorn figure of the play's protagonist, alone, abandoned, in the midst of the stripped and deserted circus grounds, with no possessions but his memories and his dreams. Presently he steps out, recedes, diminishes, and we know that by his nature he is inexorably doomed to chase the horizon beyond which he finally disappears.

IV

THE MASTER OF REVELS

OF late years there has sprung up a new profession, that of the Artist-in-the-theatre. He is something more than an art director in that he is also a creator of the entire *mise en scène;* he gives the play its physical embodiment; that is, he designs the scenery, costumes, properties, determines the lighting, and is responsible for *every thing* that meets the eye. Although his profession is a new one now, it appears to have existed in Shakespeare's time, for the duties and qualifications of the office are not different from those of the so-called Master of Revels under Queen Elizabeth, if one may judge from the following contemporary statement, quoted by Thorndyke in his Shakespeare's Theatre:

The chiefe busynes of the office resteth speciallye in three poyntes, in makinge of garmentes, in makinge of hedpeces, and in paynting. The connynge [i.e., knowledge] of the office resteth in skill of devise, in understanding of historyes, in judgment of comedies, tragedyes, and shewes, in sight of perspective and architecture, some smacke of geometrye and other thynges.

[30]

The intrusion of this functionary into the theatre of today has disturbed the even operation of the machine. It all began when the brilliant and iconoclastic Gordon Craig threw his metaphysical monkey-wrench into the works. Since then there has been a great confusion of ideas on the whole subject, the result of a confusion of ideals on the part of the young invaders of a temple which each is trying to make his own.

But these ideals and experiments must after all be antagonizing on to the establishment of a new equilibrium from which will emerge something of value for the theatre. Such at least is the not unreasonable hope of every thoughtful and sincere worker in these fields.

In order to escape from the vicious circle of mere passing fashion — each new mode effacing the one before it and then being itself effaced, like wave-marks on the sand — all effort, whether of destruction or construction, should be referred to some body of ideas, some philosophy, in point of fact, capable of withstanding time's erosion, and concerning which there can be a common agreement, even between embittered and embattled advocates of This versus That.

Were it not my belief that there is such a body of ideas, that a beautiful necessity rules this particular human activity no less than others where its sway is more acknowledged and felt, I should as soon be running a roulette wheel as working for the theatre — worshipping, that is, not the god of Order, but the god of

Chance. The purpose of this essay is to state what I conceive to be fundamental in this field.

To avoid misunderstandings it is necessary first to define this theatre about which we are talking, because there is not only the permanent and ephemeral theatre of Gordon Craig's classification, but there are all the different ideas about the theatre held by individuals, well indicated by a New York reporter's remark to Copeau at the end of one of his lectures: " I thought I was coming to hear about the theatre, but you did nothing but talk about the Salvation Army." Let us define the theatre as the home of the drama, and let it go at that. What the theatre may *become* is not considered in this definition and does not enter into this discussion, because we must start with *the known*. It is quite conceivable that the theatre may become something quite other than the home of the drama in the strict meaning of the word, that it may put the actor to new uses, or even eliminate him altogether, that it may dispense with *mise en scène* as we now understand it, and reject every formula less vital and flexible than life itself. But for the present purpose such flights of the imagination are profitless — in laying the foundations we should not be thinking of the *flèche*. It is the theatre as the home of the drama which is our present concern.

The state of the drama, though it deeply concerns the artist in the theatre, is not after all in his department, and need not be discussed here. He must assume the drama's existence, and his problem then becomes how best to make the form show forth the content — how to make the production bring out the play's every value most movingly and truly, in other words. That this is the essential function of the artist in the theatre can hardly be a matter of dispute. To be sure, it makes him the servant of the dramatist, the servant also of the actor, if we accept Stanislavsky's dictum, " The only king and ruler of the stage is the talented actor." But this idea will be irksome only to the egoist, intent on the high places at the feast; it will not worry the true artist, who knows that " all service ranks the same with God," and is content therefore to be a servant in a house where all are servants — the dramatist and the actor no less than the most humble menial who closes the doors and cleans the stalls.

It is salutary for the artist in the theatre to realize at the outset the subordination of his function, nor need he be disconcerted by such realization, for in any work of art which achieves *unity* all factors and functions are equally important. Copeau said the resolving word in summing up an impromptu debate on the importance of *mise en scène,* when he declared that the thing of real importance was that every person involved should know his job and do it well.

Let the artist in the theatre therefore face the fact that all that is *necessary* to the rendering of drama is the proverbial " three boards and a passion," that the

[33]

two greatest living all-round men in the theatre, Copeau and Stanislavsky, have shown an increasing disposition, based on a growing conviction, to depend more and more on the actor and less and less on *mise en scène*. This also is the mature judgment of Robert Edmond Jones, who says of actors: " The designer's sole ambition must be to affirm and ennoble these mystical protagonists."

Accepting, then, the play and the actor as the *given* things, how shall the artist in the theatre serve these " mystical protagonists " best? What thing is of the first, of the next, and of the least importance? Logic compels the answer that the thing of greatest importance to the actor is the thing that is *nearest* to him, most intimately his own, most personally related — his costume, in point of fact: it goes where he goes, takes the light as he takes it, a part of himself, perpetually under observation. The conclusion is inevitable that the designer's first and most absorbing preoccupation should be with clothes, endeavoring to make them so psychologically true as to create instantly for the eye the same kind of illusion as the actor is trying to build up with speech, carriage, gesture. Hamlet's " inky cloak " identifies him for the spectator before a word has been spoken: he is already a figure of doom, a stalking-horse of destiny. In the same way Cyrano's great hat with tumbling feathers, like the comb of a cock ready for battle, keynotes the manner of man he is, and the mood of the entire first act.

Next in importance to the actor's clothes are the things

THE MASTER OF REVELS

he has and handles — " hand props " in theatrical par-
lance — the book, the box, the sword, the dagger, involved with him in the action. These at certain moments
become centers of attention — centers about which the
whole plot sometimes revolves, as in the case of Emelia's
strawberry-spotted handkerchief. For this reason they
should be most carefully considered with respect to their
design, size, and absolute appropriateness — as psychologically " right " as the costume. Next in the scale of
relative importance come " stage props," the furniture
of the scene — rugs, draperies, chairs, tables: those
things which the actor contacts more or less casually,
and from time to time. Then, at the bottom of the scale
from the point of view of being most remote and removed from the actor, is the scenery itself. This should
never be thought of as other than an *environment* and
as a background, for such, of necessity, it is. It should
form, as it were, the accompaniment to the action. Now
the merit of an accompaniment is that it is at all times
subordinate to the singer and to the song. For " song "
and " singer " read " play " and " performer," and the
relation of the scenery to the drama and the actor is
accurately defined. The scenery should *enrich* the action
in the same sense that the piano enriches the voice; it
should be so good that it can be forgotten, or to put
the matter a little more accurately, the scenery should
be so designed and defined as to remain always *below*
the actors and the action in the spectator's consciousness.

But this is true only in regard to the theatre as the home of the drama — when dealing, theoretically at least, with great plays and great acting; in the field of burlesque, vaudeville, musical comedy, and the like, the above dicta would not necessarily apply, and might even suffer reversal; for it is clear that an absurd and inconsequential theme, presented by actors of two-dimensional intelligence, would be vastly benefited by a gorgeous and self-assertive production; for the eye at least, if not the mind, would be gratified. Therefore our last conclusion might be conditioned as follows: the scenery should sink, so to speak, into the subconscious, in proportion to the intensity and significance of the dramatic action.

This is easily said, but not so easily accomplished. The Moscow Art Theatre Musical Studio, in their productions of Lysistrata and Carmencita and the Soldier, employed the device of making the scenery a scaffolding (not a scaffold!) for the actors, whereon they disposed themselves to the utmost possible dramatic advantage, in the vertical dimension as well as the horizontal; then, in proportion as the scene became more and more peopled, the scenery sank more and more into insignificance, and at certain crises of the action there was " a cloud of witnesses around " eclipsing the painted and constructed background, and reinforcing the work of the principals in an altogether extraordinary way. This device was alternated with another, of more common

[36]

employment: the great spaces of the stage and all dis-
turbing details were shrouded in darkness, while the
action unfolded in a pool of light.

Light is the most important agent at the command of
the artist in the theatre for achieving the equilibrium he
seeks, and for inducing the appropriate psychological
mood. Most people have no idea to what extent they are
affected by differing qualities of light, which can be
stimulative, sedative, recuperative. The intensity, quality and color of light are factors all the more powerful
because they are only felt, not fathomed. It is impossible
to play a comedy scene with the maximum of effect in a
cold or dim light, because the spirits of the audience
are so depressed that it is harder for them to reach the
boiling-point of laughter. On the other hand, it is a
risky thing to attempt an act of tragic violence in a full,
warm light, for if the least thing goes wrong it is apt to
be received with laughter. The audience does not know
that it is affected by these means in these ways, and least
of all does the actor know that it is being so affected.
The average actor has the idea that he is being best
served by the artist in the theatre if the footlights and
borders are all at full, and as many spotlights as possible
are concentrated on himself; he thinks that everyone at
all times should see the whites of his eyes. He does not
realize that at times he would be far more effective if
strongly shadowed, or even seen as a dark silhouette
against a lighted sky, because by these means a mood

would have been induced favorable for the reception of the particular speech or action. A single example, out of a great number, will illustrate the truth of this.

In the play Othello everything leads up to, and descends from its climax, the murder of Desdemona. As produced by Walter Hampden that scene was played in a single off-stage spotlight so placed as to cast the ominous and gigantic shadow of the murderer first on the floor, then on the blood-red curtains of the bed. In a very literal sense the coming event cast its shadow before it, and vastly enhanced the tensity of the crucial moment, although it is doubtful if many in the audience really *saw*, in the sense of realizing, this shadow; they *felt* it, however, not as a part of the scene, but as power on the part of the actor.

In general, however, the actor is right in his insistence on being seen; the light on his face should be clear, natural, and constant as to color; otherwise he will be cheated of his due effect. The best lighting is that which can be most readily forgotten, on account of its essential rightness, just as we never have to think of daylight or the sun. There are of course some plays to which this dictum does not apply in all strictness, and in every play there is apt to occur a situation now and then, which calls for an unusual effect of light. Such an exceptional scene occurred in Arthur Hopkins' production of Launzi, Molnar's play of sacred and profane love, designed by Robert Edmond Jones. His problem was to get an acting

light on a passage between two people, without destroying the effect of a dark night and a dark river in which
a girl had just tried to drown herself. He solved it very
naturally and cleverly by having the action take place
in the shaft of light from the lamps of an unseen automobile, the near presence of which was called for and
explained by the play itself.

The production and control of light has reached a
point of development far beyond the uses it is ordinarily
put to in the theatre. With the right equipment it is possible to get light of any color, any intensity, anywhere;
things can be revealed or concealed by the mere throwing
of a switch. This makes possible a stage-craft of an altogether new sort. It would seem that by its aid the stage
may burst the bonds of its picture-frame altogether —
from the sides of which the actors now pop in and out
as in a puppet-booth. With light, as with God, of whom
light has been in all religious literatures the chosen symbol, " all things are possible." The drama may unfold
itself, not in two, but in all dimensions, unrestricted by
any confining boundary, beheld as it might appear to a
crystal-gazer from the recesses of his mystic sphere, or
as in the inner eye of the mind. Indeed, with the aid of
light, the theatre may be the nursery of a new art-form
altogether, a synthesis of sound, form, color, and mo-
bility, but as far removed as possible from the machine-
made things mothered by the moving-picture industry
which also involve these elements.

[39]

V

PLEASURE PALACES

WHEN John Cowper Powys was asked, at the close of
one of his lectures before a small-town Women's Club,
" If you were given a million dollars what would you
do with it? " he answered without a moment's hesitation, " I would build Pleasure Palaces." At this most
unlooked-for reply, the good ladies, in whose minds the
word " pleasure " seemed to have connotations vaguely
scandalous, were greatly taken aback: it was the inspired answer of a poet, and they had become so used
to dusty and uninspired answers that this came to them
with something of a shock.

Mr. Powys then went on to develop his idea: those
pleasure palaces would be free to everybody, their use
would be encumbered by no burdensome restrictions,
they would be open day and evening, for young and old,
rich and poor, Jew and Gentile, Protestant and Catholic,
caste and outcast. There would be recreation and amusement to suit every variety of taste — gymnasia, baths,
swimming pools, play rooms, game rooms, reading
rooms, rooms for rest and meditation, a vast floor for
dancing, music rooms and a music hall, and a completely
equipped and endowed theatre in which performances

would be given every night. The plan would include also a roof garden, an ice rink, and indoor and outdoor restaurants where the food would be both cheap and good. But above all these buildings must be beautiful with none of the institutional smear about them — that frugal and niggardly spirit to which the emptying of the alabaster box of precious ointment seemed mere sinfulness and wastefulness.

Now I believe in this idea of Mr. Powys' because I have seen it realized — only in some measure and for a limited period, it is true, and under circumstances and conditions highly exceptional, but realized nevertheless. The Red Cross Community Club House at Camp Sherman, Ohio, during the time it lasted — it was built in twenty-two days and destroyed by fire after a brief but sufficient and sufficiently glorious life — came so near in many respects to Mr. Powys' conception of a pleasure palace that a brief description of it may not be amiss.

The Club House was built just outside the cantonment limits, thus establishing, at a stroke, the entire and instant levelling of all military ranks and regimentation — the colonel and the private could meet there — and did meet — as man to man, and " Judy O'Grady and The Colonel's lady " as woman to woman. All paradoxically, the ideal of a social democracy achieved this realization in the very home and cradle of the most ironbound autocratic and hierarchical thing in the world — an army organized for war.

The plan of the building was cruciform, two hundred feet long in each horizontal dimension, and lofty in the right proportion. The interior was divided — like a cathedral — into side aisles, nave and crossing, with galleries and mezzanines so arranged as to shorten the arms of the cross in its upper stages, leaving a many-windowed clerestory from which the light filtered down, in tempered brightness, to the floor. The *bones* of the structure were everywhere in evidence, and a main element of its beauty, by reason of the admirable, direct and logical arrangement of its posts and trusses.

Entirely aside from its æsthetic interest — based upon beauty of organism almost alone — the building was notable for the success with which it combined and co-ordinated the diverse functions of a ball-room, a theatre, a restaurant and a lounge. The vastness of the interior made both for privacy and for sociability, for there were cosy carpeted oases furnished with leather-covered sofas, wooden and wicker tables and chairs, surrounding the smooth yellow desert of the dancing floor.

The appearance and atmosphere of this " pleasure palace " were pleasant and inspiring at all hours, but particularly so in the evening, when thronged with soldiers and civilian guests. The strains of music, the hum of voices, the rhythmic shuffle of the feet of the dancers — these eminently sociable sounds mingled and lost themselves in the dim spaces of the roof like the sound of many waters. Tobacco smoke ascended like incense, blue above the prevailing green-brown of the crowd, shot here and there with the brighter colors of the women's hats and gowns in the kaleidoscopic shifting of the dance. Long parallel rows of orange lights, grouped low on the lofty pillars, reflected themselves on the waxed floor, imparting to the entire picture an incomparable tone.

It seems inconceivable that the men and women who had participated, even casually, in this unique and varied social life, should not have tried to re-create it by the erection of similar buildings in their own home towns, but nothing of the kind appears to have happened; on the contrary, community life, on its recreational side, seems on the wane. The community chorus movement, so strong now in England, has died out here, the place of its origin; the theatre is being swallowed up by the moving pictures, no more a substitute for it than a gallery full of photographs is a substitute for the paintings they represent. However rude and crude the old-time small-town theatre may have been, it was a place of warmth and brightness, and the actors were at least human beings, made of flesh and blood, not their gigantic simulacra, quickened into galvanic action in a glaring parallelogram at the end of a long vista in a dimly lighted hall. These are not pleasure palaces, but lethal and torture chambers, presided over by some owl-eyed monster of darkness, not the blue bird of happiness.

Hospitals, insane asylums, jails, these we provide because we must, but Youth threatens us with no contamination and points no pistol at our head, therefore Youth is not served. By this neglect we cheat ourselves, our children, and " we despoil the unborn." Look at the situation right here in New York: not only are there no new playgrounds and recreation centers being established in congested areas with a constantly augmenting population, but many of those now existing are being preempted for other things: once-beautiful Union Square for the past two years has looked like a city dump; in Park Avenue, where old folks used to sun themselves, children play and lovers wander, there are now only iron railings and traffic lights. The grass of Stuyvesant Square is protected by iron palings as high as a policeman, Gramercy Park is a locked garden except for its sustainers, and the torrent of traffic through Central Park is so terrific that the place is no longer the safe haven for children that it used to be.

I do not contend that these changed conditions are not inevitable — that the traffic need is not after all the most pressing — but these losses should be compensated for in some other manner: by utilizing unused roof spaces, by converting the inside of city blocks into playgrounds, or by providing regional pleasure palaces. Then, perhaps, we should not need to spend quite so much money on hospitals, insane asylums, jails.

THE WORLD OF MEN

VI

ELEVATORS

I HAVE witnessed the inception of the telephone, the electric light, the automobile and — naturally — the airplane. To this list I might add the passenger elevator, for surely that black walnut-lined, gold-striped, velvet-upholstered, mirror-adorned and gas-lit cubicle which used to ascend inch by inch from the lobby of the Powers' building in Rochester, New York, to that city's crowning pride, the Powers' Art Gallery, must have been among the earliest of these contraptions. At all events it was one of the city's sights, a nine-days' wonder to the populace and visiting firemen. Mothers would take their children up in it as an especial treat; farmers from the surrounding countryside would ride in it so that they could boast to the folks at home that they had done so; and young people patronized it as they would a roller coaster or a merry-go-round — simply for the thrill of the thing. Little did anyone realize in those days that this device would add another dimension to our cities, and revolutionize their architecture, for the elevator is more the cause than the effect of the skyscraper — it is the very piston of the machine.

A. S. Eddington, in his The Nature of the Physical World, asks the reader to imagine the physical conditions which would prevail in a falling elevator: an apple, dropped from the hand, would remain there, because the hand which released it would be falling as fast as the apple fell; all weights would be expressed by the term zero, and gravitation would have become a meaningless word. Does the fat lady descending from the fourteenth floor ever reflect, one wonders, that at least for the period of her transit she would tip the scales at the longed-for figure without sacrificing a single chocolate cream, even though on her upward trip she would be correspondingly heavier? When I intend my mind on these ideas I can actually detect myself changing weight in an elevator, and feel the clutch of that old devil, Gravity, as he reclaims his victim at the bottom of the shaft, sometimes with a yank so powerful as almost to send me to the floor.

All of the fellow-passengers in a moving elevator are in what is called, in the terminology of Relativity, a different "space frame," a separate world in which the most ubiquitous of all natural forces is in a measure and for the time being broken down. This singularity I have sometimes sensed in the form of a kind of waking nightmare wherein I imagine that presently the car and all its occupants will crash through the roof and fly never-endingly out into inter-stellar space, or else continue to plunge down, down, down, burying itself,

[48]

like a falling meteorite, deep in the bowels of the earth.

A fraction of every day is spent in elevators by every city dweller: he is herded and confined as are cattle in freight cars; but in this captivity he is at least free to chew the cud of contemplation, and I never tire of speculating as to who my fellow-passengers may be, what they are " really like," and from what social or economic stratum they may have come. Like Sherlock Holmes, the most trivial indices lead me to my deductions, which are probably more often wrong than right, though as to the bandit-browed bootlegger with a heavy dress-suit case, the Captives, the Osrics, the Daffodils and such like — " Elementary, my dear Watson, elementary! "

I am so keen on this guessing game, the sole resource of the cribbed and herded, that the opening of the elevator door for the entrance of some Unknown arouses the same order, if not the same degree, of pleasurable excitement I used to experience at the opera when the festive villagers, having harkened to the legend of the castle, told in recitative by old Michael or Gaspard, turn up stage with joyful cries and gestures, awaiting the young lord of the manor, who comes that day to his majority, or the chatelaine of the chateau. To be sure in my case the lord of the manor usually proves to be only another bright young bond salesman, or a butter and egg man from the West, and the chatelaine of the chateau the free female American aborigine, Miss

No-afraid, in her wampum and her war paint, intent upon the pleasures of the chase, when not some prematurely faded virgin schoolma'am on her holiday. But after all, it makes no difference, because they will have vanished forever from my ken before my interest in them will have had time to cool.

In an elevator the life of man seems to accelerate along with the physical motion — the Sacred Fount exhibits a tendency to gush. An entire tabloid drama can be — and sometimes is — enacted between the first floor and the fifteenth. Unity of time and place is imposed by necessity, the action is largely static and subjective, the situations are scantily prepared for, and the big scene takes place, usually, off-stage. The only fully developed, complete and self-contained elevator drama with what is called a whirlwind finish was written by my friend Gelett Burgess in the days of the dinkey magazines. It was called What Is The Shortest Possible Time? and the argument runs as follows:

He and she, strangers to one another, enter an elevator together. She flashes on him a dazzling, dentifricial smile. He loses his heart to her at once; hers is already given — and to him. The car starts: in a state of beatific bliss, as though on wings, they ascend past floor after floor, their passion mounting like the mercury in a thermometer. Will they get out at the top floor? Parting would be too terrible, they dare not risk it, together they will remain, since no angel with flaming sword

drives them from their paradise. The door slams, the
descent begins, swift, vertiginous. The motion is at last
arrested suddenly, violently, throwing her on her knees
at his feet. She clasps her hand to her mouth with an
inarticulate wail, neither of fear nor pain, but of hope
destroyed, despair most desperate. Frozen with horror,
he gazes in fascination at the floor, steps over the sixteen
ivory relics of her smile, and flings himself out into the
street — alone!

The captains of these cubicular craft, containing so
much of precious human freight, are for the most part
a poorly paid, unorganized, and constantly shifting
body, operating without public control, or official license.
The position of elevator operator is usually regarded
as a stepping stone to something better, if only because
few occupations can be considered very much worse.
Nevertheless among this slicked-haired gentry I have
encountered gallant souls: eaglets, chained by the leg
within a cage, condemned to do the flutterings of the
bat. Now and then they rattle their fetters — unpack
their heart with words. Once in a great department store,
at a crowded hour, with an atmosphere oppressively
feminine, I was ascending to the top floor in an elevator
manned by one of these smouldering young Lucifers.
At each stop he was required to recite a catalogue of
what the floor contained, disembark his passengers,
and answer countless — usually foolish — questions:
" White goods, corsets, stockings, lingerie! Watch your

step! Don't get out until the car stops! No, madam, the diapers are on the floor below " — and so on. Arrived at last at the Men's Department, I was the only passenger remaining. " Gee! but this is a sissy job! " he said, more to himself than me.

There was an elevator man in an apartment house I used to frequent who spent his leisure moments, which were many, in the perusal of books of philosophy — Kant, Spinoza, Bergson, Schopenhauer — it was less a predilection than a passion. The house was favored by flappers and the male of their species, and some of them honored the elevator man with occasional and casual confidences. On the morning of some crucial gridiron battle in the Yale Bowl, one of these said to him, in answer to some comment on her early start: " Yes, we always try to get started early, because the boys take us from one fraternity house to another for the cocktails and the eats. Then we go to the game, but by that time I'm so pie-eyed that I don't know half the time what it's all about." Whereupon she joined a waiting coon-skinned, horn-rimmed undergraduate in a bright yellow sport car, while my friend resumed his interrupted reading of Spengler's Decline of the West.

The pilots and patrons of freight and factory elevators betray a different psychology from those frequenting passenger elevators. Manners are more free and speech more racy and Rabelaisian; there is more wise-cracking and rough-housing, and a more specialized and informed interest in sporting events of all sorts, particularly in what Paddy — who ran the elevator in a factory I used to visit — always referred to as "foits." He was an undersized young Irishman, probably tubercular, whose intellectual horizon appeared to be limited to the twenty-foot ring. He paid me the compliment of assuming that I was familiar with the names, records and life histories of all the gloved gladiators, and whenever I entered the car he would throw aside the sporting page with such comments as, " I think the naygar'll eat him up," or " I hear that Sharkey's goin' back." " Going back where, Pat? " I hazarded. I shall never forget his look of withering contempt.

There is a well-worn phrase, " the wit of the staircase," which is now superannuated, because nobody uses staircases any more, and wit — that kind of wit — is dead. But the correlative phrase, *the humor of the elevator*, has come to have, with me, a very real meaning, which anyone with open eyes and ears will readily understand.

VII

AMONG OLD BOOKS

In Rochester there was an old book shop where I often used to go to smoke a pipe after lunch. It was in a basement, as every well-constituted book shop should be, but there were two windows to the street wherein were shown stained old steel engravings of American statesmen in histrionic attitudes — The Signers of the Declaration, Lincoln and His Cabinet and the like — together with old books, piles of shabby magazines, ancient deeds and indentures elaborately engrossed on parchment, and articles in brass, glass, pewter and china, rescued from rubbish heaps, perhaps, to grace the cabinets of collectors.

The place was low-ceiled, dim, a little dusty and musty, but the old bindings with which the walls were lined gave it an incomparable tone. The faint glow of the embers of an open fire in some dark alcove is needed to complete the picture, but candor compels me to say that the place was heated by a cast iron stove. My friend the Bookman had formed for himself a little office by surrounding with shelving a space only large enough to hold a chair and a table for work, and an old steamer

[54]

chair for relaxation. Convenient to the hand was a box of churchwarden clay pipes and a jar of bright Virginia tobacco the color of tree calf. Here, snugly ensconced with book and pipe, " while sitting still I have travelled far."

The Bookman made a specialty of local Americana, and a chief feature of his business consisted in buying libraries from the executors of estates. He culled out such books as had real value and converted them quickly into cash, and relegated the others to the shelves to await the casual purchaser, for he had a theory — comforting to authors — that there is no book published for which there may not some day be a demand. The shop was therefore a stagnant backwater of the literary tide, full of the weedy flotsam and jetsam of the shallows. In collections of this sort certain books are almost always to be found, their dingy physiognomies becoming at last as familiar to the haunter of old book shops as the faces of habitual small criminals become known to the police court judge. The most inveterate are Festus, Deck and Port, Mrs. Hemans' Poems, Tupper's Proverbial Philosophy, and Rollin's Ancient History. The Life of Kossuth and Margaret Fuller Ossoli come next, while American Female Poets and The Capture, Prison-Pen and Escape are seen often enough to give them a familiar air.

One shelf was entirely given up to the Keepsakes, Tokens, Beauty Books and Friendship's Offerings which mark so curious a phase in our literary history. They were bound in red, black or purple cloth, stamped with florid designs in rusty gold, and were usually embellished with "elegant engravings" in mezzotint or copper-plate of ladies unbelievably and fatally fair:

> I dare not look upon thy face,
>   My bark is in the bay.
> Too much already its soft grace
>   Has won from me delay.

The verses were for the most part from the pens of the gifted "female" writers of the day, and oscillated between the lachrymose and the guilelessly amorous, abounding in allusions to "dells," to "doves" and "loves," to "flowers" and "bowers":

> The wind is playing 'mong the bowers,
> Stealing sweets from all the flowers.

Hope, Memory, Friendship, Filial Piety and other abstractions in all the bravery of capitals stalk across the pages, the subject of passionate apostrophes:

> Unclouded shone Hope's brilliant beam
>   With bright, celestial ray,
> And like a lovely fairy dream
>   My young hours flew away.

The verses and pictures were liberally interspersed with prose contributions on a great variety of subjects, all treated sentimentally. In The Ladies' Wreath an essay on Female Devotedness was followed by a story,

The Fatal Revenge, in which were narrated the fortunes
of " Celestina, the first beauty of Granada, an orphan,
and the heiress of a large fortune." A single quotation
indicates its quality: " ' Oh heaven, is it you? Is it
Celestina or an angel who has taken her figure? Ah,
'tis thee! ' cried he, pressing her in his arms."

Of a somewhat different order were those books, belonging to the same period containing practical advice
and moral guidance to young men and — more particularly — to young women: The Young Lady's Guide
to a Harmonious Development of Christian Character
and The Young Lady's Companion and Token of Affection, by the author of Botany of the Scriptures and
Wonders of the Deep. Most useful of all must have been
The Behavior Book, a Manual for Ladies. In it we are
told that " to listen at door cracks and peek through
keyholes is vulgar and contemptible," and that " nothing should be sucked or gnawed in public." The author,
Miss Leslie, is frank in her estimate of the limitations
imposed by sex: " Truth is, the female sex is really
inferior to the male in vigor of mind and strength of
body. It is well for a woman to desire enlightenment,
therefore let her listen as understandingly as she can,
but refrain from controversy and argument on such
topics as the grasp of a female mind is seldom capable
of seizing or retaining." She has one chapter entitled,
Conduct to Literary Women, telling in detail what de-
portment is proper " on being introduced to a female

writer," and the succeeding chapter is Suggestions to Inexperienced Authors: "There is some economy and much convenience in buying your paper by the ream, having first tried a sample," she says, and then enters with great gusto into a discussion of pens, inks and paper-cutters — " the best are those of real ivory."

The inscriptions, names, dates, "sentiments," written in faded ink on the yellowing fly leaves of these shabby and forgotten volumes, like the epitaphs on the moss-grown stones of a churchyard, seem to possess the power of putting the sympathetic prowler into momentary rap-port with the evanished past — the days of crinoline and Piccadilly weepers, waterfalls and Dolly-Vardens, when Byron and Elizabeth Barrett Browning kindled the enthusiasm of youth, when Ben Bolt and Captain Jinks were sung and whistled, when Dickens and Jenny Lind were popular idols and when Lyceum Lectures were the current form of entertainment.

A copy of Night Scenes from the Bible carried me, in imagination, to the sealed and garnished parlor — sacred to company and to dull Sunday afternoons — familiar to my impressionable boyhood, for this book was a chief ornament of the marble-topped center table, whereon it lay in state beside the family Bible, sur-rounded by bits of coral, sea-shells, geological speci-mens, and ancient daguerreotypes in stamped leather cases. Above the table hung a " castle in the air," and disposed about the room were the black walnut whatnot, the slippery hair-cloth sofa, the shining sheet-iron stove, and an asthmatic little melodeon, the peeling veneer and broken yellow keys of which showed that it belonged to a still earlier time. The golden summer sunshine filtered into the darkened room through the slats of the closed blinds in a stillness which made audible the hum of the bees in the lilac blossoms, and the tap of the breeze-blown branches against the sides of the house.

The book shop was occasionally invaded by comets from outside that solar system of which the rosy stove was, as it were, the central sun. I sometimes heard there the precise utterance of DeWitt Miller, and the cracked laugh and comedy voice of Francis Wilson, inquiring of the Bookman's assistant for an unexpurgated edition of Mrs. Hemans' poems. E. S. Willard left his autograph on the plastered wall alongside of a Liverbone Goop done by Gelett Burgess according to the canons of Liverbone art in its best period — which was during the reign of Ut II, who invented winking, we were gravely told, and below the twisted little figure the poet laureate of Goopland had inscribed the following couplet:

> I couldn't do this if I tried,
> But one has to curl up when one's fried.

Each honored guest was supposed to write on the plastered wall his own appropriate epitaph, and of them all I think that this, written for Burgess by Oliver Onions, was the best:

MERELY PLAYERS

When the tale of my life shall at last be told,
   This may you read of my mortal span:
I've cracked my bottle, I've spent my gold,
   I've kissed my woman, I've struck my man.

I may not close this random record of books, of moods, of memories without telling about the strangest case of bibliomania I ever encountered. In the book shop I often used to meet a shabbily dressed laborer with cracked and toil-stained hands, whose way of handling books was that of a fond mother with her child. One day the Bookman told me the little that he knew about him. The man was a mere digger of excavations for telegraph poles, receiving for his work a dollar and a half a day at most. Without ties and without other ambitions, his one consuming passion was rare books, coins and engravings. By the exercise of a frugality which imposed the severest asceticism, he was able not only to acquire a valuable collection, but to afford a trip to New York once or twice a year, where he was known to dealers and collectors.

Was it heredity, was it karma, or just some chance-acquired taste that decreed that this man be alike tormented and consoled by the love of these fine flowers of leisurely living, of the cultures of times past?

VIII

THE PURPLE COW PERIOD

THE Purple Cow period of American letters is synchronous with the Yellow Book period in England; that is, it corresponds to what is now referred to jeeringly by the Younger Generation as the Gay Nineties. And in sober truth this is not such a bad title, for the most characteristic literary products of that particular decade were inspired far more by the play-spirit than are those of today. The era found perhaps its most acute expression in certain periodically issued, small, and for the most part short-lived, brochures or broadsides referred to in the slang of the day as the Dinkey Magazines, each of which expressed the attitude and point of view of an individual or of a group. In the aggregate they can be characterized as " young," devouringly egocentric and self-assertive, and either good-naturedly or bitterly critical of one another. They constituted a sort of metaphysical Fleet Street, extending from coast to coast.

Of these magazines The Lark, The Chap Book and The Philistine were perhaps the most outstanding. The Lark, launched by Gelett Burgess, Bruce Porter, Ernest Peixotto and other talented young San Franciscans was easily the most original and brilliant of the lot, and its fame spread around the — literary — world by reason of that piece of pure nonsense, The Purple Cow, which Burgess contributed — picture and verse — to the very first number:

> I never saw a purple cow,
> I never hope to see one,
> But I can tell you anyhow
> I'd rather see than be one.

This quatrain, followed by others in the same strain of irresponsible nonsense, was worn so threadbare by continual reference and quotation, that Burgess supplemented it a year or so later with this valedictory:

> Ah yes, I wrote The Purple Cow,
> I'm sorry now I wrote it,
> But I can tell you anyhow,
> I'll kill you if you quote it!

Another of these engaging whimsies, illustrated as they all were by a humorous line-drawing, went as follows:

> My feet they haul me round the house,
> They hoist me up the stairs,
> I only have to steer them
> And they rides me everywheres.

We were always out for one another's scalp in those days, even when friendly Indians, and this quatrain I paraphrased in The Philistine with a burlesqued Burgess drawing and under it the legend:

THE PURPLE COW PERIOD

When I draw pictures for The Shark
   I do not have to think;
I let my fingers chase my pen
   And my pen chase the ink.

My first encounter with Burgess took place in the
office of the art editor of Harper's Magazine. I had just
made a poster for Du Maurier's The Martian, which had
a purple-violet sky for a background, and an obvious
association of ideas prompted the editor to remark,
" Wouldn't you like to meet the author of The Purple
Cow? He's right in the next room." So presently I was
introduced to just such a saturnine and sad-looking individual as would fulfil the popular ideal of a professional
humorist, in which the clown-with-a-breaking heart tradition is deeply ingrained. We became fast friends from
that hour, and it is to Burgess that I owe my first initiation into the mysteries of that fairyland of mathematics,
the Fourth Dimension of Space, for, like Lewis Carroll,
his mind is preëminently mathematical, and he had been
educated to the profession of engineering.

Since that time Burgess has put away the gay humors
of his Lark period, though some of them still survive
in his books for children, but in his younger days he
delighted to " put an antic disposition on " to the bewilderment of strangers and to the delight of his friends.
One night, while we were coming away from a particularly dull and bromidic dinner given and attended by
" society's true ornaments," he exclaimed, " Claude,

this is one of those evenings when I wanted to tip over the lamp! " When I asked him what he meant, he answered, in effect, " Why everyone was just bound up, tied hand and foot, by convention: no one permitted his reality to peer even for a moment out. Now if I had only tipped over the lamp it would have released us all: each would have shown himself in his true character by his reactions, whether of indignation, fear, heroism, or what not. I was just as bad as the rest of them because I lacked the necessary courage. To be sure I might have burned up the table-spread, and I would never have been invited again, but at least we would have had a moment of excitement, we would have had the taste of reality — of life."

To get the " bite " out of each moment, and to incite others to do the same, was Burgess' particular preoccupation at the time I knew him best. I could give countless examples of his whimsical humors. One night at a party in a New York apartment he sat down at a desk and wrote a letter, addressed the envelope, affixed a stamp on it, and then opened the window and threw it out. When asked why he had done such a ridiculous thing he answered nonchalantly, " Oh, some fool is sure to come along, pick it up and put it in the nearest postbox! " This proved him to be a practical psychologist, for the letter reached its destination, just as he said it would. He capitalized his knowledge of human nature to a much more profitable tune on his first visit to England, when his vogue was at its height. What he did was to borrow six hundred dollars, and invest it all in the most faultlessly fashionable London clothes that he could buy. So accoutred he visited the editors of all the magazines for which he was ambitious to write, and talked of nothing but the dinners and receptions to which he had been invited and the noble lords and ladies it had been his privilege to meet, representing that he was in London merely for pleasure, with no idea of making money by his pen. He had accurately gauged the depth of English snobbism: the scheme worked to a charm, and he ended by being implored and even competed for, to write those contributions upon the acceptance of which his very existence in England had to depend.

The Chap Book started as what today would be called a "house organ," that is, it was a side-line enterprise of Stone and Kimball, Chicago book publishers. Herbert Stuart Stone and Ingalls Kimball were Harvard graduates with leanings toward literature and the fine arts, and they decided to try to bring more of both into the business of publishing. As they were highly intelligent, sufficiently rich and excellently well-connected they met with a certain measure of success in this endeavor. On their list of authors they had Stevenson, Henry James, Verlaine, Maeterlinck, Santayana and others scarcely less distinguished, and they raised the standard of commercial book printing and binding from a low level to one which has not been transcended since.

[65]

During their régime the poster art in America entered its first and most brilliant phase, inaugurated by Edward Penfield's revolutionary and beautiful series of posters advertising Harper's Magazine. Stone and Kimball followed suit with a number of Chap Book posters by Will Bradley, Frank Hazenplug and myself. We also designed their bindings and contributed drawings to their little magazine. I have the first bound volume before me now: the rubricated title page, with its quaintly set and curiously worded sub-title and its imitation old wood-cut representation of an eighteenth century dandy with stick, stock and monocle is as witty and elegant a piece of typography as one could wish. Aubrey Beardsley never made a more decorative drawing than his illustration of Poe's The Masque of the Red Death here first published. Meteyard's title page drawing for The Ebb Tide, in point of pure design, puts the book jackets of today to shame. Bertram Goodhue, Eugene Grasset and Charles Ricketts are also represented by drawings. The letter press is no less distinguished. Among the poets who contributed are Bliss Carman, Thomas Bailey Aldrich, Richard Hovey, William Vaughn Moody, William Sharp, Louise Chandler Moulton, Josephine Preston Peabody and Paul Verlaine, and among the contributors of prose Alice Brown, Anatole France, Louise Imogen Guiney, Pierre La Rose and Richard Henry Stoddard. The Notes in each number, written or collected by Bliss Carman who was the editor, are exactly what they should be, fresh, pointed, epigrammatic — the following is an example:

> No wonder that science and learning profound
>   In Oxford and Cambridge so greatly abound,
> When so many take thither a little each day,
>   And we see very few who take any away.

In 1895, during my *Wanderjahr*, I encountered Stone in London and I went to live in a quaint little old hotel in a once fashionable square where he and some of his friends were staying — one of those hotels where the night porter hands each guest a lighted candle in a pewter candlestick to go to bed by. They all dressed for dinner every night, ordered their waistcoats by the dozen, went to parties and the opera, slept late, breakfasted in bed on toast, tea and fresh strawberries, beginning their day at about the time that I, who had risen early and breakfasted frugally, was finishing my task of making measured drawings at the South Kensington Museum. Returning thence on top of a bus I would sometimes catch a glimpse of Stone through a Piccadilly club window. This symbolizes the social and economic gulf which yawned between us, easily bridged, however, by Stone's truly democratic spirit and our genuine regard for one another. His acceptance of a drawing of mine for publication in The Chap Book was the first recognition of that particular side of my talent received by me from any source.

The Philistine was entirely different both from The

Chap Book and The Lark. It made no pretense to beauty of typography and the cover of coarse paper was of the same particularly ugly brownish-green color as present-day army uniforms. It was the speaking-trumpet, so to speak, of Elbert Hubbard — " Fra Elbertus " — pungent, abusive, witty, knowing, vulgar. Hubbard apparently dramatized himself as a sort of composite of Ralph Waldo Emerson and William Morris but his chief claim to fame is that of being the Father of Modern Advertising. He had a perfect genius for publicity, smoking up other people's talents and throwing them away like a daily newspaper, but accomplishing a certain amount of good in the process, for to his vast clientele he sustained something of the relation of Chautauqua, disseminating about as rich a brand of culturine as the middle-class American stomach was able to stand.

Hubbard's now historic dinner tendered to Stephen Crane, whose star was just then rising above the horizon, provides a perfect example of his method of getting publicity for himself by means of others. I do not impeach Hubbard's sincerity: he admired Crane's talent as sincerely as a lover the woman he desires, but that dinner, held in a private room of a Buffalo hotel, is still a distressing memory — like the sight of a young ox led to the slaughter. At first the dinner was dominated by a lot of drunken pseudo-reporters, who had come there with the evident intention of turning the whole affair to ridicule by their ribald and irrelevant interruptions, much to the distress, naturally, of Hubbard and us others. When these men were finally cowed into some semblance of order Crane was forced to his feet to respond to Harry P. Taber's tribute to " the strong voice now heard in America — the voice of Stephen Crane." What he said and the impression he made was thus succinctly reported in the Buffalo News the following morning:

Mr. Crane responded modestly and gracefully, saying he was a working newspaper man who was trying to do what he could " since he had recovered from college " with the machinery which had come into his hands — doing it sincerely, if clumsily, and simply setting forth in his own way his own impressions. He is a young fellow — twenty-four — with a smooth face and a keen eye and doesn't take himself over seriously.

Since its recession so far into the past, perhaps I am inclined to romanticize the Purple Cow period of American letters, wherein I used to be referred to as " the Beardsley of America." Nevertheless I cannot but think that it contained something precious which was later lost. William Dean Howells was its most eminent figure; A Message to Garcia was acclaimed a masterpiece; people were persuaded by thousands to believe that there was nothing to choose between a limp-leather Roycroft Little Journeys and a Kelmscott Chaucer. It was the time when the Gibson Girl put her mint-mark on the imagination of all adolescent youths, and Richard Harding

Davis was read by multitudes of nubile maidens with accelerated heart beats and retarded breath. New York was brownstone, and the Century Magazine — not a Reuben sandwich — was a national institution. It was the Age of Innocence, and it was Golden — before the sinking of the Titanic, the San Francisco earthquake and Armageddon inaugurated the Great Distrust.

IX

A PUPIL'S TRIBUTE

(Harvey Ellis)

HARVEY ELLIS was a genius. This statement may excite
only incredulity in the minds of the many who never
heard his name, and even of the few who know him only
by his drawings and paintings, but it will have the instant concurrence of those who knew the man himself.
There is the genius which achieves, and the genius which
inspires others to achievement. Had it not been for the
evil fairy which seems to have presided at his birth and
ruled his destiny, Harvey Ellis might have been numbered among the former; that is, he might have been a
prominent instead of an obscure figure in the field of
American art; but even so, he exercised an influence
more potent than some whose names are better known.
I do not know how many of the strong-nerved young
draughtsmen of the middle west nicked the edges of
their T-squares in the vain effort to reproduce his
" crinkled " pen-line — the product, had they only
known it, of nerves unstrung by drink — but it was
more than one or two; and I have seen artists of far
greater prominence bending over his water-colors in the

effort to discover by what means he imparted to them the depth and richness of a Persian rug.

My acquaintance with him dated only from the time when he was reaping the harvest of his ill-sown earlier years; when worldly success had forever passed him by; when already, though he did not know it, disease had entered and entrenched itself within the body's stronghold; and when, his two brothers having been stricken by it, madness loomed before him as a dread possibility. And yet it was to him that I and others turned for the solace of good talk, brilliant wit, wise counsel, and for inspiration and instruction in the arts of which he was so admirable a master.

He was slightly under medium height, gracefully and compactly built, and of erect and soldierly carriage. His clear, grey-blue eyes — thoughtful, serene, perceiving — looked out from beneath a delicate, high white forehead; his nose was well-shaped, but not large; a long, drooping moustache concealed a not altogether pleasant mouth set in a somewhat heavy jaw. His dual nature, that of the embodied intelligence and of the amiable epicurean touched with animalism, thus found objectification in his face. His hands were small and fine, the forefinger of the right hand stained yellow by cigarettes, the thumb phalange too small for a man who would leave his stamp upon the age. He had the dress, bearing and manners of a gentleman; there was a certain quiet dignity about him, and I think it was never

" The Odyssey " by Harvey Ellis.

more present, nor better became him, than in that crowded public ward of a city hospital to which (before his friends rallied to his aid) he had been taken, mortally stricken.

To paint an authentic human portrait pretty, bright colors will not suffice; it is the shadows which tell the story, and one dark shadow, already outlined, I must proceed to block in at once. During the major portion of his working life Harvey Ellis was a victim of drink. But I hasten to correct and complete the picture with this high light: on a certain day of a certain year — a day too long delayed, alas! — he rose from his besotted bed and for a period of ten years did not touch alcohol until, a few months before his melancholy death, weakened by disease, he sought its aid to give him strength for his daily task.

He had no more conception of the value of money than a child: he never gave it serious consideration. During the period he worked for architects Eckel and Mann, of St. Louis, he never knew what salary he was getting. When he found his pockets empty he went to them for more money, and got it — he left all keeping of accounts to them. L. S. Buffington found it necessary to deal with him on a somewhat similar basis: he gave Harvey, at the end of every day, amounts varying from a quarter of a dollar to several dollars, and whatever the sum, in the morning it was gone. The prize money which he won in the first New York Grant Monument competition he dissipated (with the help of boon companions) in three days. He seldom sold a picture because he could not endure the patronage of the wealthy buyer, while if a true connoisseur expressed a liking for one of his pictures, Harvey usually insisted on making him a present of it.

I crave the reader's indulgence if I continue to refer to Harvey Ellis by his given name, for among his friends the practice was universal. " I never had but one office-boy who didn't call me Harvey," he once said; and then after a little added, in his solemn drawl, " That one called me Harve! "

Although Harvey possessed the power of inspiring loyalty and affection in others, I believe that he himself had little real capacity for friendship. His friends chose him, rather than he them, and the burden of sustaining the relation was theirs also. I think he was the most impersonal person I have ever encountered. He never discussed his personal affairs, they seemed scarcely to interest him. He was what Schopenhauer calls " the knower, the pure subject of knowledge ": the manumission of the intellect from the service of the will seemed, when I knew him, to have taken place, and with it the predominance of thought over volition. The only things he seemed to care for were to paint cryptic, unsalable pictures, under a still north light, with plenty of time and plenty of cigarettes, and to talk about anything under the sun except himself to anyone who would listen.

Of his art I shall have something to say presently: his gift of talk deserves more than a passing mention. It made him sought after outside those circles whose interests were preponderantly æsthetic; and not only in the studio, but in the café, at the club and at select dinner parties — wherever, in fact, the conversational rose is wont to put forth blossoms — he was easily and without effort the center of a charmed attention.

It is a perilous thing to attempt to transfer to the hard, uncompromising black and white of the printed page the vaporous and many-colored flora of the conversational depths and shallows; like sea anemone, they fade and wither out of their own proper medium, but a few examples of Harvey's power of repartee may not be amiss. I remember that when the talk had turned to music, a heated argument arose on the subject of the wedding march from Lohengrin. Grierson contended that such an obvious, almost trivial melody, following so close upon the involved and sonorous music which had gone before, was an anti-climax and bad art. Harvey held the reverse, and to enforce his point said, " There are different kinds of climaxes: did you ever go into a boiler foundry noisy with a hundred hammers, and then hear them stop one by one — *and the foreman say a few words?* " There was a thoughtful quality about his wit, a knowledge of life and of human nature, manifested in such remarks as, " It's surprising what a poor statesman McKinley will be thought to be if there's a drouth in the west this summer." He was adept at framing aphorisms which appeared more true the more they were pondered. Such were, " Chairs were made to sit in." " Go sketching with your hands in your pockets." Sometimes he indulged in sheer nonsense, as in his manner of telling me that I was probably wrong when I took a swarthy American for an Arab: " His knowledge of Arabic is confined to the numerals." " George is so sympathetic " he declared, " that he'd have *delirium tremens* in a cornfield." After he had overcome his besetting weakness he was able to be funny about it. I complimented him on looking so young: " You must remember," he answered, " that I have been preserved in alcohol for twenty years."

His wonderful memory and his power of mental assimilation enabled him to talk convincingly on almost any subject, though no one could discover where he picked up all this special knowledge which was probably more wide than deep. For an American he had unusual literary tastes. He loved the Latin poets, and Dante, Malory and Chaucer. He was fond of folk-lore, Icelandic sagas, Buddhist *jatakas,* Froissart's Chronicles. Fairy stories were his delight, particularly those of Andersen and Grimm. He preferred the leisurely, discursive, old-time manner of writing to the clipped and nervous style of this later day. Among moderns, William Morris was his favorite author.

His taste was Gothic rather than Classic — that is, it

was the taste which instinctively prefers the gargoyle to the caryatid: vital ugliness to moribund beauty, the organically imagined to the artificial and arranged. Indeed it was from him that I first learned of the classification of minds into Gothic and Latin, which Gelett Burgess also popularized under the names of Sulphite and Bromide in his Sulphitic Theory. "There's one type of mind," Harvey remarked, "which would discover a symbol of the Trinity in three angles of a rail fence, and another which would criticize the detail on the Great White Throne itself." Symmetry (the love of which is the sure index of the Classic mind) was his particular abhorrence. "Not symmetry, but balance," he used to say.

I shall not discuss his architectural achievements; it would be absurd to claim much for an architect who has not left a single notable building to his credit, although there are buildings done by architects he worked for in which his fresh invention may be traced. There could be no better statement of his particular case than that made by The American Architect in an editorial published shortly after his death: "Mr. Ellis was one of those brilliant draughtsmen, full of sympathy for all the artistic part of architecture, who are, apparently, repelled by the modern practice of the profession and prefer to devote themselves to drawing beautiful architectural compositions, leaving to others the task of carrying them into execution." He was a " paper " architect, incapable of realizing in ponderable form, his architectural imaginings, and therefore cannot be numbered among the Nimrods of the profession, who with toil, amid difficulties and dangers, know the stern joy of conquest over gravitational law and earth's stubbornest materials. Their order of effort was foreign to his essentially supine nature: he plucked the flowers and avoided the nettles along the primrose path of art. For this reason he was at his happiest in problems unrestricted by utilitarian considerations, and the design he made for L. S. Buffington, in the competition for the Cathedral of St. John the Divine, stands as his finest achievement.

One may praise, without qualification, his architectural pen drawings. They are everything which such drawings should be: unlabored, economical of line, brilliant, beautifully balanced, with far more of color and body than are usual with pen drawings. His early experience as an etcher doubtless accounts for his mastery over this difficult medium.

The key to an understanding of Harvey Ellis' evolution as a painter, as it is to Whistler's, is the Japanese color print; and since I have coupled the names of these two men together I cannot refrain from calling attention to the similarity and the contrast in their work and in their lives. Both were educated at West Point; both showed, while there, an extraordinary aptitude for drawing; neither graduated; both were etchers, both painters, both wits, the center of a group of admirers, yet

[78]

The Sidney B. Coulter Library
Onondaga Community College
Rte. 173, Onondaga Hill
Syracuse, New York 13215

how different their destinies! Whistler was the darling dandy of London society, the first artist of his time, refusing more commissions than he accepted. Harvey, the Beloved Vagabond, had nothing of all this; his dearest wish was a wall to decorate, and even that was denied him.

Whistler was of course incomparably the greater artist in point of achievement, but the two men stand on something approaching an equality in the kind and degree of influence they exercised on their immediate circle of contemporaries. They represented and disseminated an order of æsthetic ideas which they found excellently embodied in the wood-block color prints of Japan. Anyone who doubts that this was the source of much of Whistler's inspiration has only to compare his Chelsea Bridge with the Hokusai print containing exactly the same elements — a bridge, a boat, a bursting rocket — similarly arranged. His famous butterfly signature, also, was the nearest approach that he could make to the decorative ideograph used by Japanese artists.

When I knew Harvey he was just in process of succumbing to the spell of Oriental art. He studied his collection of color prints to such purpose that he came to see everything *à la Japonaise* — in terms of pattern and denuded of shadow; that is, in its permanent, rather than in its ephemeral aspect. And as his eye became less of a camera and more of a kaleidoscope his art became less and less realistic and more *patterned*. The most valuable

thing these preoccupations did for Harvey was to eman-
cipate his color-sense — the divine part of his manifold
talent — from the trammels of a slavish fidelity to the
actual. His subjects were often pretentious and ill-
chosen, his compositions mannered, his drawing sometimes careless to the verge of puerility, but his color was
never wrong, and it became clearer, fuller and more
sonorous with the passing years.

He was not only an artist, he was that totally different
thing, a theorist about art. How helpful his formulæ
would have been without his intuitive sense of color and
composition is a question, for theory in art is usually
useful only to the man who is able to dispense with it;
as Schopenhauer says, " The concept is unfruitful in
art." Nevertheless no sketch of the man would be complete without reference to his theories, because they
reveal the workings of his mind.

Like so many others of a mystical and speculative
turn of mind, he was much preoccupied with the correla-
tion between color and music, based on the correspondence between the seven colors of the solar spectrum and
the seven notes of the diatonic scale. He carried this so
far as to work out color triads which should be the cor-
relatives of chords in every one of the major and minor
keys; though what practical use he ever made of this I
do not know. He tried to make of every one of his paintings something in the nature of an acrostic — capable,
that is, of being read (on its technical side) in several

different ways: first, as a pleasing line-composition (in
ink); second, as a *notan* — light and dark — composition (in charcoal); and third, as a color composition
(in aquarelle), each developed in the order named, and
superimposed on one another, just as the masters of
Renaissance painting are said to have drawn first the
skeleton of their figures, then the muscular structure as
a preliminary to the painting of the flesh. His color
composition became, in turn, an acrostic within an
acrostic; all the colors of the spectrum must appear
in it, and in approximately the same proportions, though
this principle of proportion had reference not to the
relative area occupied by the different colors, but to the
amount of pure pigment, the small areas thus tending
to become vivid, and the large areas dull. A duad or a
triad showing as a principal element was a subordinate
element as well, but modified, in the latter case, into
some new relation of light and dark, of cold or warm,
the whole thing being a concrete working-out of the law
of consonance, or correspondences, expressed in the dictum, " As is the great, so is the small."

I shall say nothing of Harvey as a teacher — though
he was my best teacher — as an etcher, or a worker in
stained glass, for my aim is, in this partial portrait, to
give a recognizable sketch of one of those ill-starred
and unrewarded fishers for that " Tyrian shell " bearing the dye of dyes which Browning, in Popularity
makes the symbol of that magical beauty revealed in an

[81]

earlier day and through a different medium in the poetry
of Shelley and Keats:

> Hobbs hints blue, — straight he turtle eats;
> Nobbs prints blue, — claret crowns his cup;
> Noakes outdares Stokes in azure feats, —
> Both gorge. Who fished the murex up?
> What porridge had John Keats?

X

THE FIRST AMERICAN MODERNIST

(Louis H. Sullivan)

WHEN the history of American architecture shall come to be written with any degree of finality, there are at least two men, the omission of whose names and achievements from such a history would render it not only incomplete but incomprehensible. Henry Hobson Richardson is one of these men, and Louis H. Sullivan the other. Each, by the power of his personality and the vitality of his genius, exercised a distinct influence upon the national architecture. In the case of Richardson this influence, although widespread, has been ephemeral. Sullivan's influence, on the other hand, though at first more limited and feeble, has been and is, of the two, much more far-reaching and abiding, for reasons presently to be explained.

Richardson's buildings though richly picturesque and possessing splendidly architectural qualities were far from practical, and the so-called Richardsonian Romanesque style, with its rough stone walls, small, deeply set windows, squat columns and round arches with enormous voussoirs, was affected, extravagant and ill-adapted

[83]

to modern needs and conditions. Being first of all a practical people, and architecture being first of all a practical art, a short time after death had put an end to Richardson's activities and so diminished the force of his
example, we abandoned the use of a style which offered
so many impediments to comfort and convenience, and
we turned to the interrupted task of adopting, adapting
and distorting classical forms and arrangements to serve
new purposes. The hope of a distinctly national style,
with Richardson as its *avant courier*, remained unful-
filled.

There was need of a new prophet in our architectural
Israel, and to the eyes of a little circle of devotees in
Chicago, he presently appeared in the person of Mr.
Sullivan. His first manner was scarcely different from
that of his precursor, but he soon developed a style of
his own, which straightway became that of a number of
others (with a difference of course) — young and eager
spirits, not fettered by too much knowledge and discipline — not fettered, indeed, by enough! Outside this
little circle Mr. Sullivan was either unknown, ignored or
discredited by those persons on whose opinion reputa-
tions in matters of this sort are supposed to rest. Engaged
upon intensely utilitarian problems in an intensely utilitarian city, Sullivan had no opportunity to captivate
the popular imagination as Richardson had captivated
it in his Trinity Church, Boston.

It was not until the time of the Columbian Exposition,

[84]

Louis H. Sullivan

when the firm of Adler and Sullivan had already gained for itself a position of prominence in the business world of Chicago and in the architectural profession at large, that Sullivan's genius obtained public and general recognition from his peers. The European architects and commissioners of art whom the Exposition had attracted to our shores, with what seemed to many of us then strange perversity, admired Adler and Sullivan's Transportation Building, relegated to the back yard of the Exposition, in preference to the Peristyle and the other highly classic confections which constituted the Court of Honor. These men had seen classic architecture before, and better than we could show them, but the like of the Transportation Building, the Auditorium Hotel and the Schiller Theatre they had never seen. They marveled at these, and admired them. The hard-headed investors who had employed Messrs. Adler and Sullivan to build for them economical, practical and rentable buildings had entertained an angel unawares: their buildings were everything that had been demanded, and they possessed a new kind of beauty as well.

In speaking of the work of the firm of Adler and Sullivan as though it were solely·Sullivan's I would not be understood to minimize Adler's part in it, which while their partnership lasted was quite equal in importance, but of a different kind. Adler was the organizer, the engineer, the business man, and Sullivan was the artist and designer. In most architectural partnerships the work divides itself up in some such way, because architecture is both a business and an art — a book bound, for convenience, in two volumes. On the other hand, I would not lead the reader into the further error of supposing that Sullivan was lacking on the side of sound construction, for after Adler's death he planned and carried out engineering operations involving originality, skill and daring.

An appreciation of Sullivan's architectural work is made easier by some knowledge of his aims and ideals, for he held views, he cherished a faith, he promulgated a philosophy of which his buildings were in some sort an expression. These views, that faith and that philosophy he set forth in magazine articles, in addresses to architectural students and to his professional colleagues, also in conversation with his friends. He conceived of architecture not as a thing to be mastered by book-knowledge, a thing of tradition and precedent, but as a living language of thought and emotion, infinitely various and free. He believed that a building, like a living thing, should be organic, eloquent, dramatic, not composed according to set rules or outworn formulæ.

The æsthetic problem presented by the tall office building, which at the beginning of Sullivan's career was just beginning to become insistent, was, to the architect educated in and wedded to the pedantry of the schools, an impossible problem. He apparently had no conception of the necessity for re-shaping his design in accordance with the change which had taken place in structural method: the substitution of a steel frame with a masonry veneer for walls of solid masonry. Accordingly he continued to try to make his buildings *look* massive in proportion to their height, to achieve which he committed himself to expanses of wall surface where practical necessity demanded windows; to deep reveals, casting dark shadows, and, in general, to a system of *seeming* supports, in the form of engaged columns and pilasters, where there was need for none. Sullivan was among the first to realize how profoundly the substitution of steel for masonry construction should affect the *design* of a building, and he was *the* first to dramatize the new structural method in any authoritative and eloquent way. To him the skyscraper spelled opportunity, and not — as to the architect enchained by precedent — frustration. Its loftiness, so far from being an embarrassment, was an inspiration; it offered " one of the most stupendous, one of the most magnificent opportunities that the Lord of Nature in his beneficence has ever offered to the proud spirit of man."

In order to understand the quality and the degree of Sullivan's success in this field — a success which revolutionized skyscraper architecture — the conditions governing the problem of the modern office building must be briefly stated. In the last analysis it is a hive, a system of cells — hundreds of similar rooms, superimposed and side by side, all equally desirable and equally lighted, as far as possible. It must be lofty, because while its horizontal dimensions are limited by the size of the lot, and the size of the lot by the cost of land, its vertical height is limited only by its stability, and the stability of a steel-frame building is enormous, for it is really a truss planted upright. The steel framework must be protected from the corroding action of the elements, and particularly from fire. The building should have as much natural light as possible in every part, and (usually) display windows in the lower, or so-called mercantile storeys.

Let us trace, now, by means of a typical example, in what manner Sullivan translated this thing of pure utility into a work of architectural art. The Prudential (Guaranty) Building, in Buffalo, affords a good illustration of his method, though today it is difficult to realize how bold a departure from the then-current practice this building was, particularly to minds accustomed to the empty architectural bombast of the eighteen-nineties.

"What," Sullivan demands, " is the chief characteristic of the tall office building? It is lofty. This loftiness is to the artist-nature its thrilling aspect. It must be tall. The force of altitude must be in it. It must be every inch a proud and soaring thing, rising in sheer exultation from bottom to top it is a unit without a dissenting line." In obedience to this dictum he has therefore enhanced the height by emphasizing the vertical dimension, so that seen in sharp perspective the windows lose themselves behind the piers and the eye is carried irresistibly upward to the beautiful coved cornice which crowns the structure. Believe it or not, before Sullivan pointed out a better way, architects used to design their skyscrapers in layers, like houses of cards — one colonnade on top of another and a gigantic overhanging classical cornice to crown the whole.

" The shape, form, outward expression of the tall office building should in the very nature of things follow the function of the building and when the function does not change the form is not to change." Accordingly, the first storeys, which serve a different purpose from the rest, he treated differently, but above them the windows are of the same size and are spaced equally far apart, to indicate that they light offices of the same size and equally desirable. There is beauty in variety, but there is also sometimes beauty in monotony, and Sullivan certainly achieved it here.

" The materials of a building are but the elements of the earth removed from the matrix of Nature, and reorganized and reshaped by force — by force mechanical, muscular, mental, emotional, moral, and spiritual." The exterior of the building is all of terra-cotta of a salmon-red color — or was, originally — and every square foot, almost every square inch, of this vast surface is " reshaped by force " with beautiful

" Sullivanesque " ornament, fine as lace and strong as steel, infinitely various and original. By reason of its flatness and its delicacy it nowhere assumes a prominence sufficient to detract from the severe and simple dignity of the entire design, yet at the same time seen from a distance it imparts an incomparable texture, while seen near at hand it is a never-ending joy. The ornament is a kind, moreover, exactly suited to the nature of fire-clay, for it is evident at a glance that it was modeled by the direct touch of the hand. The subdivisions of the pattern, also, have been considered with relation to the joints, so that the design divides itself up, like music, into beats and measures.

Of the Prudential Building Montgomery Schuyler has said, " I know of no steel-framed building in which metallic construction is more palpably felt through the envelope of baked clay." In it, and in the Wainwright Building, in St. Louis, built at about the same time, Sullivan may be said to have fully found himself: that is, he recognized in the modern office building an unprecedented architectural problem, which had therefore to be solved in a new way. In (what was then named) the Schlesinger and Mayer Store, in Chicago, he carried the logic of this discovery to its extreme expression. The building is an uncompromising parallelepiped of glass and terra-cotta-encased steel, frankly utilitarian, save that the ironwork of the two mercantile storeys is over-wrought with " Sullivanesque " ornament like flowers and frost, of such originality and beauty as to redeem it into the demesne of art.

These ideas, which are so obvious to us now, were regarded then as highly revolutionary. Sullivan was the pioneer of a truth which has become a truism. He was the spiritual father of whatever organic architecture has appeared since his time. Engulfed though the movement he inaugurated was in the great bromidic, imperialistic tide, it contains within itself the seeds of survival, and may put forth new roots and branches after the ebbing of that tide. Indeed, signs are not lacking that it has already begun to do so.

Because Sullivan was so marvellous a creator of ornament the misapprehension persists in some quarters that he was primarily a decorator rather than an architect. " Sullivanesque " ornament has too exclusively engaged the attention of his critics and commentators, who appear to regard it as his most important contribution to an American style. Sullivan himself was far from so regarding it: to him it was nothing more than his personal expression of certain generic laws discovered in nature, and he was chagrined to find his ornament imitated, and his architectural doctrine ignored. He says, " It would be greatly for our æsthetic good if we should refrain entirely from the use of ornament for a period of years, in order that our thoughts might be concentrated acutely upon the production of buildings well formed and comely in the nude." This word " nude," used in this connection, gives the right clue to his conception of the function of ornament as clothing, as adornment. Developing this idea he goes on to say, " We feel, instinctively, that our strong, athletic and simple forms will carry with natural ease the raiment of which we dream, and that our buildings thus clad in garments of poetic imagery, half hid as it were in choice products of the loom and mine, will appeal with redoubled power." He contends that a building, like a person, has a certain individuality which characteristic ornament, like a characteristic costume, assists in making plain.

Despite the fact that Sullivan failed to write himself in an arresting way on the skyline of any of our cities; that he left no masterpiece at which his devotees might gather, as at a shrine; and though his early promise failed to reach fulfillment, as a spiritual and intellectual force he is more alive today than ever, and, through his Autobiography of an Idea, exerts a strong and unremitting pressure on many minds. In that book he stands forth as the revealer of architectural hypocrisies and shams, the prophet and (let us hope) the precursor of a better order. He was essentially a pathfinder and pioneer, and had their characteristic qualities of faith, vision, courage, singlemindedness, self-reliance, as well as the defect of this last-named attribute: a certain intensification of his sense of self, a bitter arrogance scarce native to his essentially kindly and lovable spirit — a thing imposed on him, by his fighting spirit and the

[92]

number and strength of his antagonists. For the forest he was called upon to clear was of monstrous growth, and the lurking enemies powerful and savage.

Sullivan died on the fourteenth of April, 1924. It is good to know and pleasant to remember that he lived just long enough to see his autobiography in print, a palpable assurance that the travail of his spirit had not been in vain, but that its record would be a perennial inspiration to ardent and high-spirited youth — always his self-elected following. Turning the pages of his book with feeble fingers, Death already just outside the door, well might he have said, fronting that despot of our days,

This grave shall have a living monument!

XI

A MODERN MEDUSA

(Oskar J. W. Hansen)

THE Medusa, that snake-wreathed Gorgon's head, whose glance turned the beholder to stone, is one of those timeless symbols of the antique world with power to stir the imagination of artists long after the glory that was Greece had paled and passed away. The Medusa face in its early presentments was hideous and distorted, with widely distended eyes, bared fangs and protruding tongue — a thing to scare away evil spirits. In later Hellenic art it assumed a strange and terrible beauty, its expression of intolerable torment subdued to one of suffering forever unassuaged. By the artists of the Italian Renaissance the symbol was seized upon, along with the rest of the Hellenic inheritance, and made to serve new uses, for the most part merely decorative, though Leonardo's painted Medusa head was invested with that peculiar, profound, enigmatic — almost ironic — beauty which characterized nearly everything to which he put his hand.

And now comes a modern sculptor who takes this Medusa mask and makes it the vehicle of expression of ideas and emotions to which antiquity was a stranger, for they are the bitter fruitage of that sky-hiding tree which we name " modern civilization." He endeavors to represent, by means of this symbol, the travail of a soul " sicklied o'er by the pale cast of thought." The thing is as alien to the spirit of Greek culture as to that of the Renaissance, but so near to the modern consciousness as to seem its mirror image, an almost too public portrayal of secret convulsions of the soul of which we all are victims, though each believes himself unique and singular.

This Medusa head is the work of Oskar J. W. Hansen, a Scandinavian by birth, an American by adoption. I think I violate no confidence when I quote what the sculptor himself says about it in a letter:

You remember the Medusa never went into her convulsion except when people came to gape at her and she became the subject of adverse conversation. Then came the spasms which by their terror turned the onlooker to stone. In other words, she was unable to maintain her own consciousness intact against the ideas imposed upon it from outside sources. Is not this a common condition in the world today? People pushed from behind by the crowd psychology and the machine menace until they turn into masks fearful to behold. I tried to indicate also the serene consciousness still active in the vestiges of this struggling mortality . . .

Because I quote this pregnant passage from Mr. Hansen's letter I would not have the reader suppose that his

Medusa stands in need of any explaining, either by him or by me. Such necessity would be the index of its failure as a work of art. This mask may mean one thing to one person and something different to another, because "the mind has a thousand eyes," but its success depends in the last analysis not upon aroused curiosities or philosophical concepts, but upon the beauty of its strangeness and the strangeness of its beauty, upon its potency, in other words, to induce a purely æsthetic emotion.

Mr. Hansen is so much the artist — in contradistinction to the preacher or the pedagogue — that I even suspect that the idea which he presents in his letter came to him after, or during the time he was actively at work, rather than before he started, and that what really attracted him to this subject was something far more interior and abstract, having no relation to times, past or present; nor to conditions, ancient or modern. And were I to hazard a guess as to the nature of this abstract idea, I should say that it was the resolving of some paradox, analogous to the paradox of sculpture itself, for the sculptor's problem is how to capture and fix the evanescent, the transitory, in and by means of the hardest, the most recalcitrant though most enduring of materials; how to impart life and movement to that which is inert; how to telescope succession into simultaneity. I fancy that the attraction of the Medusa dwelt for Mr. Hansen principally and primarily in its own inherent nature, unconditioned by any of the special considerations dwelt

A MODERN MEDUSA

upon in this letter. That essential nature, as I conceive it, is expressed in the title of one of Blake's poems, the Marriage of Heaven and Hell — life and death, peace and pain, resignation and rebellion must be inextricably and indissolubly welded into a single memorable and significant image.

For in one sense, indeed, the Gorgon's head is a universal symbol, and this fusion of contradictory factors is of the very essence of life itself. If I want to see the Medusa face I need not go to look for it in galleries or museums, I have only to glance in the looking glass or out of the window and it is there. For in the reflected image of myself in a mirror I seem to discern an immortal spirit caged within the precarious and fast-dissolving mask of flesh which it has fashioned; while in the street just beyond my window, though there is ugliness and disorder, and greed in a thousand shrieking symbols, yet out of this sordid soil, manured by dollars, spring aloft great towers crowned with light, beautiful Valhallas, seeming to have more kinship with the sky than with the earth. Do we not find, almost everywhere we look, ugliness so terrible as to turn the heart in the breast to stone, shot with beauty so sublime as to set all our stoniness throbbing into life? And from this travail of the soul, this alternate freezing and burning, does not some winged thing develop, just as out of Medusa's body, Pegasus is said to have sprung?

Mr. Hansen is essentially a mystic, but with feet firmly planted in the world of reality, for there is about these things nothing nebulous or uncertain. His sense of touch is supernormally developed by exercise, just as is the painter's eye, or the musician's ear. He has the craftsman's love for his tools and his material. His manner of work reveals the power of his imagination and his mastery of his medium, for after having made a small clay model he destroys it, and attacks the marble directly with a chisel, releasing the imprisoned form, as Michaelangelo is said to have done. By means of some four-dimensional sense of form, he knows the instant he contacts the figure, and to the last fraction of an inch how far and how deep to cut.

Mr. Hansen is an interesting talker, and discourses so eloquently upon the beauty, livingness and luminosity of marble that one begins to wish for a piece of it, just to look at, and to hold in one's hand, and to wonder why women do not adorn their persons with it in preference to diamonds and pearls. He affirms that it is the second oldest material in the world, having formed the first white shell of this egg which we call the earth. Built up slowly from the once living bodies of minute organisms, it has, he says, a vitality all its own, which is wounded or destroyed by bad treatment, or the wrong use of tools, causing it to lose its inner coherence and integrity, and impairing its power to transmit light. These are, for

[98]

all I know, facts which scientists learn and sculptors discover, but Mr. Hansen talks about it all less in the spirit of an anatomist than of a lover, so that one gains from him the sense of an unsuspected esotericism in the sculptor's art.

XII

A PAINTER OF LIGHT

(Van Deering Perrine)

VAN DEERING PERRINE is a painter of landscapes passionate with color and movement, highly valued by connoisseurs, but he is also a " representative man," not in
the sense of being the leader of a movement, but because
he is possessed — even obsessed — by certain ideas not
personal, but general and generic, which are now clam-
oring for admission at all the doors and windows of our
House of Life. These give him no peace, no surcease
from labor; they are his sun by day and his moon by
night; they mingle with his paint, they push his brushes.
He is their enamoured victim. They all have to do with
movement and *light*. By means of a few strokes of white
chalk on black cardboard he makes one see the movement and weight of a dancer, or the long fair body of a
woman, edged with silvery light: one can almost feel
the breeze that ripples their garments, one divines both
the beginning and end of the movement of which the
mid-moment is so marvellously transfixed. The reason
why he is able to work this enchantment is because to
him black paper is not simply black paper, and white

[100]

chalk, white chalk; black paper is cosmic darkness, the womb of every form, and white chalk is light. Therefore he is not saying, "See how clever I am!" but "Let there be light!" Perrine is literally a worshipper of light. On every clear evening, for a period of years, he painted the sunset; I have seen him stare at the sun's disc, beyond the point of retinal fatigue, in order to enjoy the resultant symphony of multi-colored retinal images. Light *speaks* to him: once, pointing to the spectrum, he exclaimed to me in rapture, " Bragdon, that is the voice of God! "

Now the history of modern painting, considered from one point of view, shows an increasing preoccupation on the part of artists with problems of light; there has been a gradual transfer of attention from the fixed forms and local colors of objects, to their forms and colors as affected by ambient light. This preoccupation found its first concerted expression in the work of the French Impressionists, who, thrillingly aware of that opalescent atmospheric veil which wraps everything round, strove to represent objects as acted upon by light. Perrine belongs, in one sense, to this school, but pushing still farther in the same direction he strives to paint *light as acted upon by objects*. Light reveals the forms of things, but if its intensity be increased beyond a certain point it dissolves and obliterates the very forms it has revealed and pervades the space they occupied. Perrine says:

My attention was first called to this as I watched a tug and its tow enter the blazing path of light cast upon the water by the ascending sun. As the tug approached the field of brightness it began to vanish and finally disappeared; the tow, which had remained visible, now followed, swallowed up in vibrant light. I knew that they were both there, within that narrow band of almost intolerable brightness, because I had seen them enter, yet their forms were as completely lost as though they had entered the deepest gloom. Presently the tug began to emerge, and passing into the less intense light, gradually regained complete and clear definition, and the tow similarly withdrew from the invisible realm and took on form in the visible. I had been accustomed to escape from the literal through the mystery of darkness and of shadow, but here before me was proof that the same escape could be achieved through the agency of light.

The field of the painter — the field, that is, of visual perception — is bounded on the one hand by brightness and on the other by darkness; into either of these the identity of objects is swallowed up. It is at these *vanishing points,* where the invisible triumphs over the visible by reason of excess or dearth of light, that fancy is bred — here is the true playground of the imagination. Perrine prefers to present nature as she appears at these transitional moments, when a door opens into the world of the wondrous. But not for him the sable door of darkness, associated with thoughts of sadness and fear, rather the silver door of light, suggesting confi-

" Autumn Days " by Van Deering Perrine.

dence, joy, gladness and the morning of life and of the world.

His range is narrow: the same elements perpetually appear and reappear — sunlight, wind-blown trees and scurrying children — but this is due neither to his limited powers as a painter, nor as a man to lack of interest in other aspects of the world. What appears to be a perversity is really something profoundly different, for what Perrine is trying to present in all his pictures is not an " aspect of the world " at all (though anyone is free to accept it as such should he so choose) but his sense of a beauty which is universal — an *immanent divine* — expressed through and by means of a chosen set of symbols. What makes his work so different from other painters who employ symbolism, however, is that his mystical message is couched in Nature's own language, so that one is under no compulsion to recognize it as symbolism. He renders Nature at some of her most mystical moments as seen through the window of his temperament, but without a text scrawled on the pane, as it were. He presents neither his personal self nor his private opinions, but Beauty's self as revealed to him in a certain way and at a certain moment of time.

For Perrine is an incorrigible knee-bender at the shrine of Beauty and holds perpetual communion with her visible forms. He is the " meek lover of the good " who turns his back on heaven to study the mould on the

bark of a tree, the pattern of a leaf, the wing of a dragon-
fly, finding in each a manifestation of the divine; but for
him, as said before, its supreme manifestation is in
light. In the white light of the sun, containing as it does
every color, he finds the perfect symbol of the *human-
divine* — a fusion of differently " colored " individuals. Accordingly, into every one of his later pictures,
he introduces an absolute white radiance, the center and
focus of that shattered and scattered rainbow which is
the picture's self. But this whiteness, this serene efful-
gence — like Brahma, " without passion and without
parts " — fails to express the stir and strain of life —
its *becomingness* — so he supplements this symbol of
" the day's at the morn " with another which might be
called " the year's at the spring " — tossed tree-
branches, shivering leaves, wind-driven clouds, anything
suggestive of fertility, fecundity, life's orgiastic Dio-
nysian revel. And he has a particular fondness for the
figures of young playing children, hurrying, half
glimpsed, *sans* features, or with averted faces, for by
them he would suggest that shy, sweet, evasive, ecstatic
newness — Love's delight — the secret preoccupation of
all the sons and daughters of men, pursued by them, even
to the rainbow's end.

All this may seem far-fetched to those who only see
in Perrine's pictures a painter's perception and rendering of certain unusual aspects of the visible world, but
those who feel more deeply see more truly. The sym-

[104]

bolical content of which I speak reveals itself in a certain *abstractness,* a generalization of form: his children are not merely Joan and Peter, but childhood; his trees are not elm and willow, but *treeness.* To a man who asked why he did not paint trees so that they could be identified botanically Perrine replied, " If you could tell what kind of a tree it was you would think you knew its secret, but I want you to feel that the tree is a great green mystery pushing itself up through the sod and reaching up to heaven — as great a mystery as you or I."

But it would be wrong to conclude that Perrine's paintings are the result of an intellectual process, that they represent the application of a theory or the operation of a system — nothing could be farther from the truth. The man works intuitively, emotionally, from his solar plexus rather than from his cerebral center, or even from his optic nerve. Only retrospectively did he discover that in introducing and repeating certain motifs for which he had an especial fondness he "builded better than he knew."

The heedless see in Perrine's pictures only a blurr of brilliant paint; the artist easily discerns the hand of a master-craftsman; the nature-lover discovers the impassioned record of some moment when the world was touched with wonder, stirring to the imagination as a strain of music; rare souls discern in them a painted prayer. Though they are small things and slight, —

measured by inches rather than by feet — they are nevertheless *big*. This is because they meet, in some measure, the three demands of all true and enduring art: spiritual content, emotional appeal, and æsthetic form.

XIII

AN ARTIST'S LETTERS FROM CHINA

(Willard Straight)

WILLARD STRAIGHT died of pneumonia in Paris on December 1, 1918. In his thirty-eight years of life — or rather in the final fifteen years of it — he achieved distinction in various fields: art, diplomacy, international finance. His brief, brilliant career abounded in amazing antitheses and dramatic contrasts. He steeped himself in the magic and mystery of the East, thereafter to immerse himself in the social and financial vortex of Western civilization. He was in turn an illustrator, a newspaper correspondent, our consular representative in Manchuria, a member of America's most famous banking-house, an exponent of more enlightened trade relations and a major in the American Expeditionary Forces, attached to the staff of the First Army. He was equally at home in Buddhist monasteries and at London dinner-tables, yet through it all he preserved an utter simplicity and directness — he was never guilty of an assumed emotion or of a histrionic gesture.

I first knew Straight as an architectural student in Cornell University. One of the requirements in order to graduate was a certain number of months of actual experience as a draughtsman in an office. Accordingly, he applied to me for a position during the long summer vacation. These negotiations led to nothing in that direction, but established a relation which soon became a friendship. I remember him as a modest, charming boy, with a clever knack for sketching. At that time the art aspect of his manifold talent was uppermost and covered his whole sky.

Straight was born in Oswego, New York. His father, who was a professor of zoology, died when the boy was six years old, leaving the mother to provide for the two children. She bravely carried on her husband's work of teaching, and being offered a promising position in Japan, at the Girls' Normal School in Tokyo, she went there with her children, remaining for a period of two years.

He thus experienced the seduction of the East when he was very young. He woke up, as it were, in a wonderland of sights, sounds, odors, from the sweet tyranny of which he was thereafter never able to escape. A born artist, the most powerful appeal the East made to him was the æsthetic appeal. As this happened to be mine also, I encouraged him in his ambition to go to China after leaving college, and there render the perpetual pageant of the Oriental world in terms of paint; for he

[108]

saw the world at all times as the painter sees it — multi-colored, coruscating, in the camera obscura of the eye.

Not long after his graduation I began receiving letters from him from China, where, a clerk in the Chinese Imperial Customs under Sir Robert Hart [1902–4], he was soaking up the life around him like a sponge, and squeezing it out again in the form of pen-and-ink and water-color sketches of a charm and distinction which can only be characterized as rare. The following letter, adorned with spirited pen-drawings, well indicates the quality of his reaction to the spirit of the East.

" MY DEAR MR. BRAGDON,

" As you'll see, again, by the above " [a sketch of the walls of the Tartar city], " I am in the Northern Capital, Peking, most rudely torn away from Nanking and its steaming summer. But in this case I pardon the impoliteness of the Inspector General in ordering me away from my Chinese studies in the south, for he has very considerately put me at them again up here, and with a better house, better climate, and what's more to the point, better teachers.

" Then, too, I am well pleased because the place in itself, so many years the seat of empire, and latterly of the Boxer horrors, is full of ancient monuments, and, unfortunately, modern ruins. There are temples of all sorts and descriptions, tombs, and monasteries. At any time as one wanders through the crowded streets, one is likely to come unexpectedly upon some new wonder.

" Then, too, the streets themselves are great unworked mines, from an artistic standpoint. The contrasts one sees thereon: rumbling Peking carts, rattling slat-sided rickshaws, great lumbering goods wagons drawn by three or four mules, or shaggy ponies — or both, and then again, winding in and out, a string of camels, dirty, reeking with their own peculiar odor, blinking, as they pad softly along the way.

" Legation quarter itself is a veritable fortress, surrounded by a glacis on three sides, and the Tartar City wall on the other. The weary diner-out, wandering homeward in the wee sma' hours, is halted every now and then by a sentry, and must answer ' Friend,' and be told in Russian, or Japanese, or Italian, or whatever else it may be, to ' advance and be recognized.'

" The streets are policed by the troops of all nations; the duly appointed native guardians of the peace being by their own firesides, and the breakers of it everywhere throughout the Chinese City. The Russians are great, hulking fellows, bronzed and hardened by exposure and much vodka. The Japanese and English are smart and natty, our own men a bright-looking crowd, the French, undersized, dirty little beggars, the Italian and Austrian sailors a fine lot of men, but the Germans! Ai ya! Such a bargain-sale crowd I have never seen. Worse fitting clothes couldn't have been especially designed for them.

Stupid and heavy, they are absolutely the worst crowd in Peking, and, for that matter, in all China.

" I am following your advice, and sketching incessantly. I spend many of my afternoons wandering through the streets sketching and gossiping with the people, and on Sundays nose in and out among the temples, and about the country which hereabout is charming.

" There is a Spirit of the East. I feel it, all the time, and the feeling grows in me. It is indefinable yet, but there is something overpowering, crushing in its terrible strength, its disregard of human life. Here, where one falls and a hundred take his place, the Divine Spark is but a cheap commodity. There is not the Individual, rather, there is the Mass. This Essential Being is wild and ghostly — like the music, now low, now soft, thrumming, now shrill, screeching up and down the scale. It is full of self-abnegation, of fanaticism, of demoniacal cruelty, and Divine Pity, and there is a mist about it, a mist that swirls and eddies incense-laden, thinning for an instant to unveil the vision that is wrapt again, ere one can realize its full portent. And the colors are gorgeous, yet subdued and softened, the light is dim, there are the passing reds of human blood, tainting now and then the heavy incense-perfume, and there are wild bursts of song, and the wailing of stringed instruments, rising in a pæan that is yearning, yet full of an awful, irresistible power.

[111]

" It is thus that I am beginning to feel it. I can't describe it really, but some day I want to paint it. Yet even that would be a meagre rendering, for it needs the heavy air, and the wild music too. I know that there is a chance out here to learn something and to do something but the flesh is weak, and occasionally — yes, more than occasionally— one slumps, and needs a strenuous kick. That kick you can administer if you will, for as I said before, you started me off some time ago when you told me to work at the Japanese side of it all. So if you would make a good finished product of the rough material, you must stir the clay a bit now and then, and I assure you, the clay will appreciate the stirring, and the stirrer. . . ."

The next letter (also illustrated) opens in much the same strain of confidence mingled with that natural self-distrust of lonely youth craving reassurance. In his own form of words, and confronted with his own æsthetic problem, he gives voice to the ancient plaint of every sincere artist: *Ars longa, vita brevis est*. Then follows an extended description of a temple ceremony which shows his extraordinary susceptibility to the purely visual appeal — to color, light, sound, movement. His knowledge of the Chinese language, together with his sympathetic and engaging personality, enabled him to penetrate deep below the surface of Oriental life, and the temple priest, so amusingly described, who served him both as a model and as a purveyor of ancient scrolls, was only one of an almost endless procession of picaresque characters fixed by Straight's clever pencil and sensed by his impressionable and ever-curious mind. Years afterward he entertained me with the recital of adventures as preposterous, amusing and dramatic as those of Haroun-al-Raschid himself. I remember in particular one tale about the effort of himself and a friend to discover, by means of Eastern magic, the author of the theft of a valuable photographic lens. The commonest method — the questioning of an adolescent under hypnosis — having given no satisfactory result, a veritable high priest of the art of necromancy was persuaded to make the attempt. In semi-darkness, amid the most outré surroundings, after the performance of all manner of magical rites, the necromancer succeeded in evoking before their eyes a flat image — a picture — of a man with averted head. Straight affirmed to me that to his amazement and that of his friend this pictured head was then made by the magician to turn — hesitatingly, as though unwillingly — half toward them, and that it revealed a profile which they recognized as that of the particular Chinese official whom they had suspected of the theft from the first.

" MY DEAR MR. BRAGDON,

" It has been some time since I received your letter, much longer, in fact, than I had supposed, and I trust

[113]

that you will not consider my tardiness due to any lack of appreciation on my part, of your kindness in writing me so promptly. As I wrote you before of your first letter, your second was very helpful in that it started me off with an idea that there was something to be done, the goal to be reached by steady work ahead still within the range of the Possibilities, at least, and not to be considered absolutely unattainable. That is the great thing out here in the dozing East. One forgets the constant striving that is apparent everywhere at home, and is tempted to let matters run their course more or less, trusting to luck. ' And when they ain't pretendin', they are good.' Flesh is weak, and some weaker than others. In this particular case, a rather constant prodding would be most beneficial, not to say absolutely necessary. You have kindly consented to assist in the pricking process, and I assure you, I am very greatly indebted.

" There is so much to see, so much to paint, and to think about, that the immensity of the task is almost appalling. One wishes for a lifetime of bright blue days, and even then it would seem hopeless, for it could be done so well, and the technical difficulties are so hard to master and overcome. However, these may be a bit accomplished even ' in the ride,' and there's a deal of pleasure in trying.

" Of late I have been Llamaizing, I suppose you might call it, lurking about in Buddha-decked nooks and corners in the great Mongol monastery, listening to the

[114]

droning, chanting, mumbling voices of the priests —
some of them rumbling in heavy bass, others giving
their clear little boy-notes to the Song of Praise. There
is a continual dum-dum-dumming of drums, the rising
and falling notes of the trumpets, the squawking of
flutes, the clank-clank of the cymbals, slower at first,
then all finishing the measure with a terrible clash of
sound. The service finished in one side-chapel, the
Llamas file out, in their flowing crimson mantles and
their old-gold felt caps, like the horse-hair plumed hel-
mets of the ancient Greeks. These men gather about the
doorways or scurry through the courts to their cells, and
the never-ceasing hum passes on to the next chapel. It is
strange how very like the robes of the Catholic priests
the garments of the Tali-llamas are — long, flowing,
purple, with the embroidered ribands down the back.

" One Sunday morning I went early to the temple.
They were preparing for a feast, for the courts were full
of orange-robed priests; their crimson scarfs were fresh
and clean, and they wore fur caps with yellow tops and
red buttons of twisted silk. Friends of mine, from other
temples outside the city were there, looking cleaner and
more respectable than I have ever seen them look before,
and beside them were many white and blue button men,
magistrates in the city. I went in past the great bronze
lions at the gates, on into the inner temple courts, and
into the first great hall. Here was a yellow silk canopy,
covering a great map-like affair. Six or seven men were

sifting colors, red and blue and green and yellow, in lines and scrolls and broad fields. 'Twas the map of heaven, they said, and showed me the palace of Lord Buddha in the center thereof. Moving in towards the other side of the room, I looked back over the group squatting and working. Around them were a crowd of onlookers, priests in purple, officials in silks and embroidery, laymen in the omnipresent blue. A shaft of light came slanting through the doorway, bathing them in yellow splendor, and deepening the shadows. In the full light several orange-clad men were standing, and their gowns shone and whitened. Beyond was the shadow, the green-grey, picked out by the glint of gold, or a bit of red, in the garments of the painted Buddhas on the walls. Rows of idols massed themselves dimly, scarcely losing themselves in the twilight.

"Then as I stood there, drinking in the color, two Mongols, skin-clad, heavy-shod, unwashed, came slouching in, their astrakhan caps in their hands. They threw themselves on their faces before the great smiling impressive image, and prayed, their voices rising and falling, while from the chapel without came the low hum of the chanting priests. It was a picture to be painted, if there ever was one.

"Today I have been doing an oil sketch of a priest of the temple. A most disreputable individual he is, a thief and a blackguard — but useful. Already he has brought me four splendid scrolls, two of them from

[116]

Thibet, painted in a sort of oils, on canvas, faded and worn and dusty. Two of them are of Buddhas, on silk, dating back two hundred years and more, for the date is written on them in Chinese. The colors are mellowed and blended and softened by time. When I come across a good one I will send it on to you, trusting that it may be honoured with a place in your brown and orange and blue room. . . ."

The following brief letter was written at the moment when Straight was just about to forsake forever the primrose path of art for one more dusty and adventurous, leading finally into high places and among great figures. Thereafter, he was to become an actor rather than a spectator in the world-drama of West and East. He makes me his executor, as it were, in the matter of disposing of six charming water-colors of Chinese types. These suffered the fate which so often attends things beautiful and rare: though much admired by connoisseurs they found no purchasers. Whether the series was ever completed or not, I do not know, but in any case this letter marks the end of his absorption in the East as material for art and the beginning of his absorption in its political, economic and financial problems.

" MY DEAR MR. BRAGDON,

" It has been a very long time since I have written you how the Far Eastern world was turning, and as a matter of fact, any letter that I might have written would have been more of the nature of a political treatise than a bit of respectable correspondence. Our minds have been wholly wrapt up in the wonderment which the rapid course of events must have caused anyone who followed them, and which to us who are out here, of course, has been absorbingly interesting. And now as a result of this mental development, or deterioration, whichever you choose to call it, I have burned my bridges — whist! — and am off to the wars as a correspondent for Reuter and the Associated Press, with a sketch book in one hand and a pad in the other and a telegraph wire around my neck. I am off to the front in high fettle, for I see chances for much exciting experience, and many real sketches.

"I am therefore sending you six drawings of as many different sorts of Chinamen; the series I started was to consist of twelve, but some have fallen into the hands of friends and some went as Christmas presents. If you could do so, and think the subjects and the execution worthy of such a distinction, I should like to have you have them suitably mounted and framed, and sent to the American Water Color Society's exhibit or any other. My original idea, when I had hoped to go to St. Louis as Secretary to the Chinese Commission, was to have taken them there, but that now hardly seems worth while. However, I put them in your hands for better or worse, and if you could exhibit them or sell them, or

[118]

both, I should be greatly obliged. Some day I shall finish the task I was forced to drop in its more or less initial stage, and the final results may be more deserving of your consideration. But such as they are, I will turn them over with many prayers for their successful venture into the public gaze.

" I trust that you are well and are finding the life of a benedick all that the poets have claimed for that blissful state. I cannot write at greater length for I am off at a moment's notice and frightfully rushed. Thanking you in advance for your trouble, and trusting that you will not find the task a perfunctory one, I am with kind regards,

" Sincerely yours,

W. D. STRAIGHT."

The next is written on the somewhat florid letter paper of the Hôtel du Palais (L. Martin, Propriétaire) at Seoul, Korea, and bears the date of June 4, 1904. Straight is now a seasoned and accredited war-correspondent " in charge," as he says, of Korea, and contributing despatches on the Russo-Japanese War to the leading newspapers of the West, and sketches to the London Graphic.

" MY DEAR MR. BRAGDON,

" Many thanks for your kind letter. I was extremely glad to hear from you again, and to know, also, that you approved of my pictures. Your approval quite braced me up. Now this can scarcely be called the Front, though it's much nearer than most people have been able to reach. I have been here for the past three months, and if you've been reading the papers you've probably seen some of my stuff. Bare cable messages can scarcely be called literary efforts. However, it means something to have been ' in charge ' of Korea.

" I am now off on the most wonderful expedition ever arranged by any government. The Japanese are sending members of the House of Peers and the House of Commons, officials from the Foreign Office, the Foreign Naval attachés and several military men, with ten European and American correspondents to see the theatre of the war. The expedition goes on the ' Manchuria,' formerly of the Russian Volunteer Fleet, and captured in Nagasaki by the Japanese at the outbreak of hostilities. The humor of the situation is tremendous. Think of running a naval picnic in wartime, sending out sightseers by a government steamer timed to arrive at Port Arthur as the Japanese land and sea forces make their final attack. Isn't the situation attractive?

" Up to date I have done very little drawing — some sketches in the London Graphic, and that's about all. One's time is very much occupied in chasing from Legation to Legation in a wild hunt for the desired news item. However, the experience has been most interesting and I have enjoyed every minute of it. Korea is more like

[120]

a comic opera than anything I have ever seen. Some day I will write you of it — some day when I have a little more time. Just now I am busy packing Korean chests and other truck I have laden myself with during my stay here.

" I am glad to hear that architecture and magazines are booming — that's fine. One of these days I shall drop in on you again. Till then, believe me,

"Sincerely yours,

" W. D. STRAIGHT."

An interval of three years appears to have elapsed before I heard from Straight again directly. The ever more swiftly flowing current of affairs in the East absorbed his attention and his energies. By this time he had attained to the position of consul-general at Mukden, an office in which, by reason of his intimate knowledge of Eastern affairs, his tact, his ability, his scholarship, he performed distinguished service. The tone of this letter, dated May 12, 1907, from Mukden, is noticeably different from that of the others. It is more mature and reflective. His attitude toward art has changed from that of a participant to one of interested, critical observation. He has glimpsed the truth that art cannot flower in any community torn by war and trade rivalries, and he has now definitely forsworn his earlier ambitions in order to do his part toward bringing about needed adjustments. In an article on Straight, published in the

New Republic shortly after his death, he was characterized as pre-eminently a pioneer, and this is a true char-
acterization. Yet how few pioneers are called upon to
make just his sort of a renunciation — not of a country
in which life has become intolerable, but of a sweet
demesne in which his spirit was perhaps more at home
than in any other.

MUKDEN, *May* 12, 1907.

" DEAR BRAGDON —

" Now that is temerity indeed! I wonder if you know
the feeling that one has when one wonders about tacking
on the tail to a name, or letting it drop in a desire not
to be thought too formal — yet regretting the amputa-
tion as possibly an over-hasty claim of familiarity. However, I should have written you long ago, for I want to
congratulate you on being a father. It must be a rather
strange and yet a very wonderful thing to look such a
problem in the face. For it is the making of one cannot
foretell how much that is in one's hands, and the benefit
of all manner of experience that should be given, and
which one would so wish to impress upon the growing
mind, but which will, I suppose as long as we are human, be disregarded by Youth who prefers to learn from
nature and not from a parental text-book. I've often
wondered whether a boy ought to be taught to fight, and
I rather think he had. Don't you? Don't you believe that
beautiful instincts will come with age — control and

[122]

regulation — while if the natural, primitive manifestations of a desire to excel or to conquer (which in the
human male as in the other nobler animals must be exhibited in physical strife, more or less) are suppressed
and discouraged, isn't the result more apt to be a weak-
ling? And isn't it easier to control strength than to viri-
lize weakness? If I ever have a boy I think that I should
make it a point that he should never fight in a wrong
cause, or without reason, but that if he did he would
have to win! Is that Christian, or not?

"I have just re-read your letter in which you speak
of Maxfield Parrish's decoration for the Knickerbocker
hotel. I should like to see it. One admires his work
tremendously — though as you say, it is too literal, in a
way — there's no sweep of action. His people are all
mural decoration people, and not of real flesh and blood.
Yet after all is it not possible that as decoration they are
more honest and frank admissions that they are decorations — color schemes embodying natural and human
forms as the patterns?

"I should like very much to see your designs for the
leaded windows. Haven't you a rough sketch thereof
that you could send me? You've no idea how barren one
becomes in this part of the world — how much a machine — or an ambitious sponge-like being, dipping into
Treaties, and Regulations, and questions of procedure,
or policy, or trade, with never an instant hardly in which
to think even of the better things — they are higher you

know for they are enjoyed by those who have won the right to do so after having passed through all this travail which we are watching now — commercial readjustment. I mean of course from a broad point of view.

" In Italy the Renaissance came, didn't it, at a time when there was a great commercial prosperity, where the tradal relations between cities were fairly well regulated, and when war had been reduced largely to a matter of the purchase and repurchase of mercenaries. Things were more or less adjusted, and people could stop a moment to think or to paint. Am I correct? They couldn't have done these things if they were all clustering around one market, clutching at one another, squabbling and pulling over taxes and freight rates, preferential treatment, and the confusion of political design with commercial ambition — could they?

" In Manchuria, many times, it is fascinating to think of it all in the abstract, but so frequently it becomes such a reality, so near and intimate a part of life, that it is impossible to secure the necessary perspective. In a way, therefore, you who at home have your plays, and above all your music, and your telegraphic connection with all parts of the world, are in many ways more blessed than we who are way at the end — the nerves far away from the center of intelligence and sensation.

" The political problem is a fascinating one, and I wonder what you would think of the fellow-countrymen of Hokusai and Hiroshige if you knew them as diplomats, soldiers and merchants, in a land where they were preceded by folk who had little sense of the finer distinctions between *meum and tuum.* I make no comments.

"What China is going to be able to do in these troubled parts I do not know, but it will at least be interesting to see, unless some sudden changes take place in the capital, which is not unlikely. We are to have a new Governor here — a person who has graduated from Columbia — who speaks English perfectly, who has passed through the Boxer trouble, and is as a result bitterly anti-foreign — but not in the old blood-curdling style — intelligently so, I mean, with a stern resolve apparently to wound them in their tenderest spot — their pocket — by refusing any form of mining or railway concession. He is reputed to be the cleverest diplomat in China and has stood the Russians off in good stead for some months in Peking. What will happen after his arrival, I do not, as I say, know, but that something will happen we all feel quite sure.

"I am sending you some foolish pictures that may interest you. With kindest regards, and hoping to hear from you,

"Yours sincerely,

"WILLARD STRAIGHT."

The latter part of Straight's life, concerned as it was with large affairs both in America and Asia, is beyond the province of this essay, since the letters which portray this earlier phase end here. Few men touched life at so many points, and with such insight. But greater than his achievement in any field was the spirit behind that achievement, and these letters, written at a time when he had that leisure and liberty which is the precious prerogative of obscure and untrammelled youth, perhaps portray that spirit more adequately and truly than others written amid the dust and heat of the arena in which his greater battles were fought. He died young, and his career was meteoric, but he was captain of his soul — the bow and not the arrow — and the aloofness from those passions which commonly muddy the wills of men who mould the lives of other men was held by him to the end.

To me he always seemed to be one of the vanguard of that younger race which is yet the elder, by reason of its greater wisdom, detachment, artistry in life — a race destined to unite not alone the East and the West, but continents not geographical: those hemispheres of thought and feeling indifferent or actually hostile to one another now. Straight's work in promoting a better understanding between America and Asia was only the outer symbol of a reconcilement of ideas and ideals which he in his own person represented, and these are coming more and more into acceptance by free spirits everywhere throughout the world.

XIV

A MIGHTY HUNTER

(Nicholas Roerich)

My first meeting with Nicholas Roerich occurred at the time his paintings were first exhibited in New York. He had come to this country with them at the invitation of the Chicago Art Institute, and fascinated by the freshness and strength of the spiritual life which he discovered fermenting within the three measures of our materialism and leavening it, he decided to make America his home. In our very first talk we discovered that we had many interests in common: our theosophical outlook upon life — inlook would be, perhaps, the better word — the fact that we were both practically and vitally interested in the theatre and our mutual admiration of Ouspensky's Tertium Organum. He had read it in Russian, and was surprised and delighted to learn that the English translation by Nicholas Bessaraboff and myself had aroused great interest, had received commendation in high quarters and was becoming well known.

My second encounter with Roerich convinced me that we were in the pattern of one another's lives, because that meeting involved the long arm of coincidence which always means to me something quite other, something quite the opposite of what we call chance — that " man's accidents are God's purposes " I veritably believe. I was in Buffalo for a day, and I saw by the paper that Roerich's exhibition was at the Albright Gallery. Surmising that I might find the artist there also, and wishing to see his paintings again in any case, I took a car out to the park only to find the doors to the Gallery closed for the day. Disappointed in this, I decided to chance a call on my friend Spencer Kellogg whose house was not far away. This took me, straight as a homing pigeon, to the very man of whom I was in search, for I found Kellogg and Roerich sitting together in front of the fire as though they were waiting for my arrival, and had they been doing so I could not have had a warmer welcome, nor a better time.

Roerich reminds me of nothing so much as a Chinese sage: his Mongolian cast of features, his scant grey beard and moustache, his deep-set all-discerning, yet introspective eyes and his mountain-like strong serenity all contribute to this impression. One feels that he is possessed by the calm which comes only to the completely dedicated. How infrequently they are encountered, and how unmistakable they are! It has been my privilege to know a number of the members of this spiritual aristocracy whose insignia of nobility are not stuck in the buttonhole or sewed on the coat, but sound in the voice and shine forth from the eyes.

"The Miracle" by Nicholas Roerich.

A MIGHTY HUNTER

The following summary of Roerich's activities and comment on his art are taken, with the kind permission of the publishers, from the introduction I wrote to Roerich's book of travels entitled Altai-Himalaya.

For thirty-five years — ever since the time of his first exhibition in Russia — Roerich has been going up and down the world — traversing Europe, America, Asia — adventuring into remote and dangerous places, uniting his consciousness with those of diverse peoples, unearthing legends and folk-lore, and recording what his eyes saw in paintings freighted also with those meanings which his spirit divined. And wherever he went he scattered wisdom and good-will, and planted seeds of beauty, some of which have sprung up, flowered, and scattered seeds of their own.

In Russia, as secretary of the Society for the Encouragement of Arts, and later, as director of the school of that society, he was an important agent in organizing and coordinating that native, new and powerful impulse which in painting, in music, in the drama and in the dance later spread throughout the civilized world — for it is not too much to say that everything which now goes by the name of modernism (except in architecture) has had Russia for its procreant cradle. It is significant in this connection that Stanislavsky enlisted Roerich's aid in the Moscow Art Theatre, that Stravinsky dedicated to him the *Sacre du Printemps,* for which Roerich designed the *mise en scène,* and that Andriev, Gorky,

Mestrovic, Zuloaga, Tagore and others throughout the world who represent *the newness* have paid him the homage of their honor and their praise.

Roerich believes, as many others are coming to believe, that neither commerce nor diplomacy, but *beauty* is the universal and true solvent of racial and national differences, misunderstandings and animosities. With this idea in view, he founded, with the help of friends, the Master Institute of United Arts, a school the nature of which is told by its title. A year later he established Corona Mundi, an international art center. The school encountered those vicissitudes which usually attend enterprises of this character in a civilization such as ours, the best image of which would be a rush-light in a wind-swept darkness — but it survived, and shortly will be housed in its own skyscraper on Riverside Drive, the only building of its type in the world named for and dedicated to a living artist. Other vast outlines, sketched by Roerich, have not yet been filled in. They include Cor Ardens, an affiliation of artists world-wide in its scope, and Atalas, an international, non-commercial publishing association for the interchange and dissemination of new and constructive ideas through the mediumship of printing and publishing.

I mention these enterprises, realized, partly realized and unrealized, to show the vast sweep of Roerich's vision, to indicate that he is not an artist merely, but a prophet and a pioneer, clearly foreseeing and quietly planning a better order in a world still in the grip of its so terrible recent nightmare, not yet risen from a bed drenched with blood and stained by tears.

Should his dreams of binding humanity into a brotherhood through beauty materialize, it will be for this, doubtless, that he will be most honored and longest remembered, but to us, his contemporaries, he is naturally best known as an explorer, and as a painter of hauntingly beautiful pictures. These are of all kinds and on a vast variety of subjects, but in general they represent nature strained through a mystical consciousness — the light that is on sea and land translated, by some potent magic, to the light that never was on sea or land. Roerich satisfies the idealist without affronting the realist. Mukerji, the Hindu novelist and poet, told me that Roerich's paintings of the Himalayas alone gave the true impression of them, because along with the rendering of their form and color their spirit was communicated too.

It is characteristic of the man that he should have journeyed to that roof of the world, Thibet, " the sacred imperishable land." After a brief sojourn here, in obedience to some inner monition of the spirit, he forsook the ordered and easy life of cities and undeterred by the rigors, dangers and difficulties of such a quest, he set out for the Himalayan plateau, "trailing clouds of glory" so to speak, in the shape of paintings of the Grand Canyon, the Santa Fe country, the Pacific ocean,

India and the Far East. The culmination of his life
work, up to the present, is in those groups of paintings
named by him The Thibetan Path, Himalaya, and Banners of the East. These are freighted with mystical
meanings which, even though unintelligible to all save
the initiated, yet act upon the unenlightened consciousness as does perfume upon the senses, or as music upon
the emotions. It is not that Roerich attempts to be cryptic
— on the contrary, most of his symbolism is almost
naïve in its simplicity — but the average mind so re-
sents the very idea of esotericism, that it closes itself
to that order of appeal.

Roerich's symbolism, as I say, requires no glossary,
for it has the qualities of simplicity and universality.
An example of his general method is seen in that painting of the Messiah series, entitled The Miracle. It represents a titanic valley, not unlike the Grand Canyon, a
world primeval, stark, rock-strewn, without visible flora
or fauna. Prominent in the foreground is a natural
bridge, and over this bridge passes a road. On the near
side of this bridge are seen seven figures, prostrate before
the miracle of a great radiance coming from behind the
bridge, the shining aura of some supernatural presence
whose figure is not yet visible. Here is a simple, natural
symbology, subject perhaps to different interpretations,
but none of them contradictory. Considered objectively,
the picture is simply a dramatization of that expectancy
of a Messiah which is so widespread nowadays, and the

[132]

healing assurance is held forth that though His presence is not seen, His aura brightens the darkness, His influence is already operative. Considered from the standpoint of subjectivity, the denuded valley might symbolize the condition of the soul, after trials and purgations; the road, " the small, old path " to perfection and liberation; the bridge, that stage on that path where the transit is effected between the lower and the higher consciousness; the prostrate figures, those " qualities " which must be redeemed and " carried across," all awestruck at the felt approach of the " golden person " bringing release from bondage through the shining of the inward light.

But the great merit of this picture, freighted as it is with meaning — as it is the merit of all of Roerich's paintings — lies in its beauty of color and composition. The mystic and metaphysician in him never submerges the artist, with the result that when he permits himself the use of symbols he is still lyrical and not literary: his pictures are not sermons, but songs. The Miracle, despite the fact that it conveys a message, is not a morality so much as a delight to the visual sense, abounding in spatial rhythms and color harmonies as fine and subtle as those of some priceless old yellow Chinese rug. The story is there, but the final indelible impression is one of beauty and this is as it should be, for in the hierarchy of professions, trades and talents the creative artist is nearest to the throne of God.

Of Roerich's archæological pictures I shall not speak, nor of his pioneer work in the theatre, important as that has been, because I feel that these things, which at one time absorbed his mind and dominated his consciousness have since become far less important than what I shall call his *mystical quest*. One has the feeling that in everything he does he is seeking some hidden truth, some unrevealed beauty — the Lost Word, in point of fact. Like some mighty and indefatigable hunter, armed not with a gun, but with his brushes and paints, he stalks his quarry across oceans, rivers, mountains, though knowing all the while that the thing he is seeking is in himself. In this adventure he permits us to participate.

XV

THE DELPHIC MOVEMENT

(Angelo Sikelianos)

In Æ (George Russell) is incarnate the very spirit of
Ireland. The entire Celtic Renaissance, as any informed
Irishman will tell you, can be traced straight to his door
by the footprints of those whom he had inspired. Æ *is*
Ireland. Now Angelo Sikelianos stands in exactly this
relation to modern Greece: both are poets, both are
mystics, both are dedicated by an occult and irresistible
compulsion to the reanimation of an ancient culture,
the reorganization of life according to an antique pattern. The Delphic Movement is different from the Celtic
Renaissance only in so far as the spirit of Greece is
different from the spirit of Ireland: both movements are
concerned with the introduction of greater efficiency
into agriculture, the revival of handicrafts, the reëstab-
lishment of the drama as a force in human affairs —
with the effort to restore the soul and not the stones: to
recreate from the Iron Age, the Golden.

An incorrigible modernist, I have seen so many artists
and authors turned to stone by looking overlong on the
beautiful Gorgon face of ancient cultures that my first

[135]

contact with the Delphic Movement was tinged with a certain skepticism. But in this I was wrong, and my error was revealed — as so many things are revealed — in a dream.

To my dream-consciousness the salvation of the human race seemed to depend on everybody's dancing out of doors. For this there was need of a vast level floor, and in my capacity as architect, this I was called upon to provide. I straightway went to work to construct it out of wood, in a great beautiful valley, between the mountains and the sea, though knowing all the while that such a platform would be ugly, expensive and impractical; that the sun, rain and wind would so warp and roughen it as to make it soon unfit for use. In digging for a suitable foundation for the supports, however, just beneath the surface of the ground I uncovered a perfect, permanent white marble pavement, with which the entire valley seemed to be floored, laid ages ago, and for a similar purpose, so that it only had to be cleared of the top-soil to make it serve for the dancing feet of modern youth.

By means of this symbol I was made to realize that each advance into the future is a return to some long-buried past, which can be made to serve a modern purpose if dealt with from the point of view of a new and different consciousness, and that this new consciousness is indeed the Perseus shield in which the bright Medusa must be looked at if we would escape being turned to stone by ape-like imitations of ancient grandeurs, and

Angelo Sikelianos.

meaningless repetitions of *mantrams* whose inner content is no longer understood. Ouspensky says " Things are differentiated by their consciousness," and because Sikelianos in his Delphic Movement approaches the past with eyes fixed on the future, that movement is not the exhuming of a mummy, but the releasing of an entranced spirit, an evocation which might conceivably win mankind back to the quest of some new beauty, as did the rediscovery of Greek and Roman art and learning which inaugurated the Italian Renaissance, and as admiration of the Italian primitives inspired the Pre-Raphaelite movement in England.

The fact that Greece and Ireland are geographically small, economically poor and politically unimportant is of no consequence in this connection: theirs is a sacred soil, and spiritually fertile by reason of the flame which burned there long ago which, once kindled, must forever burn. Just as Ireland is reputed to be the sacred island, so the ancients regarded Delphi as " the navel of the world," the meeting place of the terrestrial and the celestial. Its famous oracle has long since fallen silent, but it need not be, for that reason, forever mute. Indeed, to ears attuned it has already spoken, and its mouthpiece is none other than Sikelianos himself. His utterances are impressive, both in weight and volume, and are well known to the cognoscenti of his own country and of Europe, but by reason of the barrier of a difference of language it is only recently that a medium of communication has been established between him and the Anglo Saxon world through Alma Reed's admirable English translation of his Dedication of the Delphic Word. This is his latest poem in point of time, having been published in the demotic, or modern Greek language at Athens in 1927. The original is written in rhymed iambic octameter couplets, and the translator has so successfully captured the spirit of the original that one has no sense of its being a translation.

The poem is deeply mystical, charged with spiritual lightning like the storm-clouds which gather about some sacred mountain. In language heavy with thought and vibrant with emotion the author recounts his vigils, his purgations, his encounter with the " Father of my Land," his initiation, his recovery of " the sacred valors," and his dedication to the cause he serves.

Sikelianos is regarded with great affection, respect and even reverence by his fellow-countrymen, who apparently feel about him much as the Irish feel about Æ. In him they divine the spirit of ancient Greece to be again incarnate; and they look to him to reëstablish that mystical empire over the hearts and minds of men which Greece once exercised, has never wholly lost, and which may be perhaps more easily established in this postwar twilight than at high noon.

XVI

A MODERN PROPHET FROM LEBANON

(Kahlil Gibran)

I REMEMBER vividly my first meeting with Kahlil Gibran. It occurred at one of those cultural tea parties so dear to the heart of the average American woman, and so abhorrent to husbands, sons and lovers. As a result the atmosphere was pervasively, even oppressively, feminine, inducing a psychic mood analogous to the physical sensation of immersion in warm water or the feel of an old-fashioned feather bed. In the waning afternoon he and I were the only two men remaining, which may be the reason why, metaphorically speaking, we so fell on one another's necks.

I do not think that at that time I had really read him, though I probably pretended that I had done so, as he possibly pretended that he had done the same by me. But this proved to be a matter of no importance: we came together "like kinsmen met a-night," finding that we spoke so much the same language that there was scarcely need of speech at all.

In that first meeting I saw him as I now see him, all later encounters having only deepened and intensified the impression received then. Three words describe him: *artist*, *poet*, *prophet*, though they should be only one word, but this the English language fails to furnish forth.

Gibran is a native of Lebanon. Now Lebanon, like Delphi, is holy ground, a nursery of prophets, one of those places where the sacred flame has never been permitted to snuff out. The Lebanites, I am told, are as different from other Syrians as the Scotch highlander is different from the lowlander — more so, indeed, because they are of Nordic, and not of Semitic, stock. His was what is called in the East a " fortunate " birth, for he was brought up in an atmosphere of love, beauty and abundance. Not only were his people affluent and cultured, but his mother's family, from far back, was the most musical in all the countryside.

The boy was extraordinarily precocious, drawing, building, modelling and writing with such absorption and avidity that his parents used to try vainly to bribe him to stop. When he was only eight, the pale presentments in books and prints of the mighty spirits of Michaelangelo and Leonardo stamped themselves indelibly upon his consciousness — " wax to receive and marble to retain." At the age of twelve his parents brought him to this country. He returned and entered a Syrian college at fourteen and a half. For a number of years thereafter conceive of him as going and coming between Europe and America, pausing long enough in Paris to learn drawing as practiced in the Ecole des Beaux Arts; always in active exercise of his twofold talent — poet and painter inextricably one.

His earlier works were written in Arabic — prose poems: Broken Wings, Spirits Rebellious, and a number of plays. These were published in the United States, Egypt and Syria, and soon made him known to the entire Arabic world, which extends — ethnically and linguistically — from China to Spain. The character and depth of his influence upon that world may be inferred from the fact that it gave rise to a new word: *Gibranism.* Just what this word means Gibran's English readers will have no difficulty in divining: mystical vision, metrical beauty, a simple and fresh approach to the so-called problems of life.

About ten years ago, in this, the land of his adoption, he began to write exclusively in English, and those ten years have been sufficient for him to create a corresponding impression upon the Anglo-Saxon world as well. The books he is known by to this world are The Madman, The Forerunner, The Prophet, Sand and Foam, to which must be added Jesus, the Son of Man, and a collection of twenty drawings without text.

These books are sparks from one fiery trail, parts of one coherent structure, the successive presentment of a simultaneity — a presentment which has by no means come to an end. For Gibran's most widely known poem, The Prophet, which deals with man's relation to his

[141]

fellow-man, is the first of a trilogy, to be followed by
The Garden of the Prophet, having for its theme the
relationship between man and nature, and The Death
of the Prophet, the relationship between man and God.
It is not possible to " get " Gibran without some sense
of these organic relations, any more than it is possible
to sense the vast sweep of Michelangelo's genius by
looking at the Sistine ceiling, panel by panel, through
an opera glass.

I do not propose to analyze these books, nor even discuss them: there they are, and each reader must inter-
pret them as he may please. Gibranism I leave to the
Herr professors past, present and to come. Some cosmo-
conception is implicit in the works of every mystic —
and Gibran is a mystic — but I am no more interested
in cosmo-conceptions than in cross-word puzzles —
which they greatly resemble — and neither, I venture to
say, is he, except in so far as some such kind of an inner pattern may help him to precipitate the particular
kind of beauty of which he is in search.

A philosophy — conscious or unconscious — is to the
author what dynamic symmetry is to the painter, or to
the builder the scaffolding with which he surrounds his
monument: however necessary to the construction they
should not be in evidence in the finished structure. Gibran's works, it is true, form a sequence; they represent
the " pilgrim's progress," each is a " station of the
cross "; but each one contains and is the whole, in the

[142]

same sense that each branch of a tree is itself a tree, and each leaf a tree in miniature. To achieve these unities is the problem of the artist, who labors to conceal all evidence of labor, and this being so, he prefers to keep such matters to himself.

The theme of Gibran's books is one with his major interest, and his major interest is in *life*. He aims to discover some workable way of feeling, thinking, living, which shall lead toward *mastery* — how to serve the forces which enslave us until they are by us enslaved. Such, I take it, is his purpose, his " message," but having said so much I should be remiss not to call attention to the extraordinary dramatic power, deep erudition, lightning-like intuition, lyrical lift and metrical mastery with which that message is presented, and the beauty, beauty, beauty, which permeates the entire pattern, with which everything he touches seems fairly to drip, as it were.

Gibran's paintings I have never seen; his symbolic drawings represent a phase of art with which I have no affinity, and therefore prefer not to speak; his portraits and ideal heads are frequently magnificent, and possess a strikingly Leonardesque quality. Like the great Florentine before him, Gibran seems to be always searching for the perfect androgynous type, knowing that in this some cosmic secret, well for men to know, lies deeply hid and preciously enwrapped.

Because the character and personality of Jesus

represent this man-woman nature in the purest and most perfect form of which we are yet aware, is perhaps one reason why Gibran's imagination has always hovered about the majesty of Jesus' teachings and the mystery of His life. He has made that life the subject of his book: Jesus the Son of Man, he calls it, and to have named it thus instead of Christ the Son of God, casts a light upon his entire attitude toward life.

To him " nothing is higher than the human " — the only supernatural he recognizes is man's own super-nature, and he has utter faith in man's power to become divine by *realization;* that is, by *making real* the divine, in the human life.

Of this process and its results he chooses Jesus as the great exemplar and he is so eager that his readers should both see and understand Him, that he adopts the device of *straining* Jesus, so to speak, through the consciousness of His immediate contemporaries, ene-mies and friends alike — each one a cloth of finer or coarser texture, in which some trait or aspect is netted, or on which it leaves an azure or crimson stain.

The cumulative effect of this method — the same that Browning used in The Ring and the Book — is enormous, and of all of the books written about Jesus, this one, if only for this reason, may be said to be unique. It is distinguished also by the varied beauty of its prose and verse, and its dramatic intensity. Though not cast in the form of a play, it shows Gibran's power of conceiving situations and creating characters which convince by their truth to human nature and their fidelity to life. One wishes that at some future time he would adopt the dramatic form more definitely. He could wield that Excalibur — and how few can!

I once went through the form of interviewing Gibran, and so asked him that most banal and bromidic of all the interviewer's questions, his " impression " of America, just to see what he would say. He answered me after this fashion:

" Conceive of the world as a rose-bush in a sky-garden, with races and civilizations for its blooms. Some flourish, from others the petals are falling, here one is withered, and just beside it, where once was a great red-hearted blossom, only an empty stalk remains to tell the tale. Now on this rose-bush America represents the bud just pressing at its sheath, just ready to blossom: still hard, still green, and not yet fragrant, but vigorous and full of life."

Beauty is to him more than a word, more than a *thing*, it is a *being*, one which may be made manifest, *material-ized* through the magical power of the combined action of the hand and the brain. He believes that Beauty blesses him who makes it thus manifest, and his sense of the reciprocal action between " the unborn, the soul that passes not away " and its shadow on time-space — the personality — he translated into the terms of his own experience in the following way:

[145]

"If I encounter a beautiful face on the street my eyes are fed, my spirit exalted, but I want to know that beauty also with my brain, and with my hand — I want to *draw* it, and if by chance I am able, I participate in it, I become part of it, and it becomes part of me. That's what always happens to the artist — all the time I was writing The Prophet, The Prophet was writing me."

His writings, his drawings, his sayings — of which the above are examples — are saturated with his peculiar quality, dyed in his soul-color; but how convey, more directly, some sense of the man himself — the noumenon of these phenomena?

Physically he is compact, strong, swarthy; all his movements are powerful and graceful; he seems charged with the dark fire of a *maleness* mitigated by the sweetness of his smile, the gentleness of his glance. His face is sensitive; one would say that it was a face of suffering were it not even more a face of peace. Buttoned underneath his coat is an ever-burning lantern; he does not mean that we should see it, but somehow we know that it is there. Only by some such preposterous metaphor am I able to suggest the sense of inner happiness, harmony, unity, which his presence projects.

One sees the same thing in adolescent lovers, but we know that with them it is sometimes so fragile as to be killed by the first frost; whereas with Gibran — though no more than another immune from those " slings and arrows of outrageous fortune " forever hurtling through this slum of space — we feel that he has touched, with invisible hands, the Immortal Beloved, has received from her mysterious favors, and experienced incommunicable delights.

On this green earth, or rather (since he lives in New York) on this gray asphalt, his feet are solidly planted, and with something of the air of the Little Corporal surveying the battlefields of Austerlitz, for though the most modest and unpretentious of men he has certain traits of the commander and the conqueror — not the commander of cohorts or the conqueror of women's hearts, necessarily, though he might be the one and may, for all I know, be the other — but the captain of his soul and the master of his fate.

He loves society as well as solitude, is an enjoyer of small things as well as great, of things physical as well as metaphysical; although he is austere in one sense, there is nothing of the ascetic about him.

All this sounds like a fourth reader description of the Temperate Man, or the Industrious Apprentice, and just here, for the uses of art, I ought to paint in a few dark shadows, but I shall have to let the description stand as it is with the assurance that he isn't, after all, quite like it — he evades me and escapes me. With that eloquence which consists in understatement Gibran once summed up his feeling about the latest work of a certain author by simply saying, " This is a *book!* "

Very well! This is a *man!*

XVII

A MID–VICTORIAN MYSTIC

(Francis Grierson)

THE letter from the manager of the Assistance League of Southern California begins as follows: " You no doubt have heard of the sudden passing of Francis Grierson in Los Angeles on May 29th (1927). Just prior to this the attention of the Assistance League had been called to the fact that Mr. Grierson was in dire need of financial aid. A plan was worked out to communicate with certain of his friends and admirers for immediate financial assistance and advice on a program for the future. In the meantime it was our privilege and pleasure to assist Mr. Grierson with emergent aid. When the tragic end came we felt that it was our duty to arrange for a funeral worthy of one who had done so much for mankind; one which would meet with the approval of his friends. We are now faced with two problems — one of meeting the funeral expenses, and the other of helping Mr. Tonner, his secretary and closest friend," — etc, etc. In brief, Francis Grierson died in poverty in the midst of the proverbial plenty of Hollywood, in ironic confirmation of the truth of his own statement " He who does not love my spiritual intelligence will not take any pains to care what becomes of my body." His friends, remote and scattered, myself among them, knew of his need too late. He indeed would have been the last to inform us, for he was proud as Cyrano, and his last phase was like Cyrano's — poor, aloof, alone, at war with all the current snobbisms, and keeping, at any cost, his own " white plume " inviolate. The last letter I ever received from him, written from Washington ten years before he died, is a jeremiad against the false artists, false poets, false philosophers who for gain and preferment drag their white plumes in the mire:

There is nothing the average mind so dislikes as originality. A poet who has failed to achieve distinction hates good poetry; an architect who can only draw the obvious hates the artist with imagination; the verbose essayist hates the concrete. Bret Harte joined a yacht club in England to get free of jealous scribblers. Yes, the American business man, at his best, has not been sounded! He is about the only *natural* individual left in this country. I could write a book on what I have recently learned, and I assure you I intend to act on the knowledge gained. It is shocking to have to say so, but the majority of the women I meet want nothing but English and foreign things. A lecturer who is English is all right, no matter what he says, and a freak pianist from Poland is certain of big audiences, no matter how old and stale his music. As for the democratic spirit in American society, it exists nowhere. The art in a thing no longer counts here; it is the person they want to see, and if the person does not possess high social connections in the old country so much the worse for that person. And it is futile to go against this awful snobbery. It pervades everything. The artist in these days who refuses to take people for just what they stand for is doomed to failure. And you and myself, and others, will have to take the world on the basis of the blank and impudent materialism on which it rests, or we shall get little accomplished while we live. Therefore, be wise! A very *grande dame* here, and one with famous ancestors, advised Waldemar [Tonner] to address the fashionable audience at her mansion, before the recital, and tell the company who my ancestors were. Think of it! You see my art, my books, my poetry would not be enough! I am telling you this for a purpose. We may live in our ideal world, but we cannot bring it into the world in which we move.

This dark view of the American scene misrepresents — or represents only partially — Grierson's habitual outlook upon life, and should therefore be corrected by the following observation from another, earlier letter:

I find a great hunger among the more serious people for knowledge of a higher order, and a great awakening seems to be at hand. I am frequently surprised at the invitations I receive from a distance from people I have never seen.

It is surprising that Grierson is so little known, considering the variety and distinction of his talents, and the length and brilliance of his career. This began in the Mississippi valley before the Civil War as a page in the retinue of General Fremont, was continued in Europe,

[150]

where, as an inspirational pianist, kings and courts contended for the privilege of doing him honor. He was a prominent figure in the hectic and brilliant social and artistic life of the Second Empire, with a Cagliostro-like reputation for the possession of strange psychic powers and the mastery of occult arts. This continental sojourn, interrupted by occasional returns to America, was followed by fifteen years spent principally in London, and during all this time he was writing profound and brilliant books, both in French and in English including The Valley of Shadows, which is considered by many who have read it to be the greatest American novel of pioneer life.* The final years of his life were spent here in the United States giving lectures and piano recitals. What took him to Hollywood and what happened there I do not know, only the stark fact of his death, read in an Associated Press dispatch, and shortly afterwards supplemented by the letter from the Assistance League of Southern California.

I came in touch with Grierson first through a corre-

---

* Among Grierson's best known volumes are *La Revolte Idealiste*, written in French and published in Paris in 1889; Modern Mysticism, London, 1899; The Celtic Temperament. 1901, which was adopted as a literary textbook by the Imperial University of Japan; The Valley of Shadows, 1909; which was translated into French, Russian and other languages; Parisian Portraits, 1910; *La Vie et Les Hommes*, Paris, 1911; The Humor of the Underman, London, 1911; The Invincible Alliance, 1913, a plea for the moral solidarity of the English speaking world; Illusions and Realities of the World War, 1918, and Abraham Lincoln, 1919.

spondence inaugurated by our mutual interest in each other's books. This was during his London sojourn. Later I met him in New York through my friend Arthur Farwell, whose interest in Grierson's strange musical gift was acute. After that we carried on a desultory correspondence, which, by reason of our so different destinies and absorptions languished and finally died out altogether — to my regret. My memory of him, however, remains vivid, and his letters I never had the heart to destroy, they are so full of wisdom and nobility.

He was a tall, English-looking person, with an old-world air about him, enhanced by the formality of his dress and manner, which were everything that one associates with the term " Victorian." He had the largest feet I ever saw on a human being, and they seemed always to be giving him trouble, so that he was self-conscious about them, just as was Cyrano about his nose. He was a brilliant conversationalist, full of amazing true stories of his adventures in various out-of-the-way corners of the world. He was reputed to possess the gift of prophecy, many times confirmed. It is certain that he predicted the war and the Anglo-American *entente* in The Invincible Alliance and he accurately forecast the trend of events in Mexico. The flavor of his mind can be tasted in the following quotations from his letters. The first one, written from London shortly before his departure for America, contains interesting information about the writing and publishing of his masterpiece:

A MID–VICTORIAN MYSTIC

Since you speak of having read The Valley of Shadows I may say that only the most clairvoyant minds can penetrate to the inner meanings of the book. The others read it as a fine novel. It took me ten years to write, and all my fortune to the *last* silver shilling. When the last page was finished the last shilling was spent. But, as you are quite able to understand, books like mine are not, and never will be, written for *money*. I was nearly two years waiting for the proper mood in which to write the portrait of Lincoln as he stood against Douglas at Alton. There is not a mechanically written page in the book. It was published four years ago and I had to part with the copyright and I was financially crippled and remain so to the present day. Mr. Lane is about to issue an illustrated edition at five shillings and a popular edition as well, but I shall never receive any money from that source, no matter what the sales may be. My ambition is to have the American public acquainted with the book and I do not regret the loss of all I possessed. I am no believer in chance. When my parents left England for America and went direct to Illinois in the midst of the great psychic movement, they had no idea why they went. My parents had not the slightest notion of what I was or what I was to do. There were no schools. No one ever taught me *one thing*. The Valley of Shadows had to be written by me, or not written at all. The fundamental reasons and conditions of that time had to be recorded in that *particular* form. But spiritists and others also must not think any portion of that book was ever dictated by any spirit. The art that is not felt is not art at all, but something else. Genius is self-conscious or it is nothing. The phenomenonalists are the gravest danger we have to face, even in this enlightened age. People who see in my music a phenomenal wonder may be innocent enough in themselves, but they are no company for me, and they will not assist me in my mission and my message, or in anything whatsoever! The spiritists are on the lowest plane of all. A spiritist regards a man of genius as a mere machine to be worked, as a slave works, and small sums of money are handed to a medium as if wisdom and inspiration could be bought like coffee. There is no virtue in anybody who is wanting in reverence.

The bitterness of his invective against the spiritist had its root, doubtless, in his own experience, for the true mystic is always being confused, by the undiscerning, with the mere medium, and pursued and preyed upon for purely selfish ends, and Grierson was a true mystic, in conscious contact with the world of the wondrous. In confirmation of this let me quote from another of his London letters:

I have been held, for the space of fifteen years, mostly here in London, and the marvels that have happened in that time would more than fill a volume. Today I spent from three to four hours on the top of motor buses, riding up and down the marvellous hills of Kingston, Putney Heath (Swinburne's favorite) and Wimbledon, suburbs of London, and I experienced a *spiritual afflatus* absolutely transcendental! I received *key notes* and directions for future work. Today, here, we have experienced an electric atmosphere such as rarely comes to London — a westerly wind, cool, with clouds, and full of psychic possibilities. Perhaps never before have I felt such a radiant and supreme domination. . . . I was in some doubts before; now, after my three hours ride in company of Gods and Goddesses my directions are quite clear and lucid. The one fundamental secret of power is that of Time in combination with indifference and serenity. I have held to that for more than *forty-three* years! Not till we renounce everything earthly do we enter the precincts of power, psychic and transcendental. The lessons are exceedingly hard and bitter . . .

In my short history of the Theosophical movement in America, entitled Episodes from an Unwritten History I had occasion to describe the first meeting of Madame Blavatsky and Colonel Olcott, the two founders of the Theosophical Society. This took place under unusual circumstances in a rude and dilapidated old farm house, once a tavern, in a remote and sparsely settled valley in the Green Mountains of Vermont, where both had come to observe the " Eddy Manifestations " then a nine-days' wonder. I learned from Grierson, to my surprise, that he was of that company and present at that meeting, about which he has this to tell:

You do well to write about the " romance " of such things. The dull people are the realists. A man is old when he ceases to wonder. When I come to write and print my account of my visit to Chittenden in the autumn of 1874 you will have still more reason to write the word *romantic*.

In 1872 I was in Russia, in 1873 in London, in 1874 in New York. I arrived in New York in the middle of August and a few weeks later found myself escorted by two of my elderly New York friends up the Hudson to Albany and from thence by rail to Chittenden without any apparent reason for my going there. I had no business there and did not much like the idea of going, but my two friends, one of them Colonel Paul

Bremond of Houston, Texas, paid all my expenses there and back to New York City and that made me decide on going with them. That made my fifth journey across the Atlantic, and I was only twenty-five. And yet there was absolutely no apparent reason for my acquaintance with anybody at Chittenden. I was not to do any kind of work with Madame Blavatsky. Now I know that a great cycle-wave was established and set in motion by the music I gave on one special evening in the big room where the manifestations were visible. I gave the music after the regular evening seance was all over. I at first refused positively, not wishing to be mixed up with the manifestations, but my New York friends insisted, aided by Madame Blavatsky. But I first made Col. Olcott promise not to write about my music in the Daily Graphic. He kept his promise but was infuriated later on when another newspaper correspondent who was present in secret wrote a highly sensational article on the music for *his* paper, and Olcott, thinking I had given this man permission to write the article felt insulted and extremely bitter. All this I learned months after the happenings, and by a friend living in New Haven. Imagine my surprise. All these are facts. The atmosphere of the *tout ensemble* I shall give in my printed recital, with my reasons and explanations, and my knowledge of the way cycles begin. It has never been done and no one is alive now who could even approach the subject from the personal contact view; most of the people who were there being middle age and over are dead, and for all I know they are all dead but me, but even if some of them are alive it would require art to put the ensemble properly before the critical reader and re-create the atmosphere, which is *ambient magic*. Besides all this the thing must have what in law is called a judge's " summing up." After I am gone no one can do it. The thing seems imperative . . . It is highly important that you should have issued these books recently! They are themes in a great symphony.

Like Madame Blavatsky herself, Grierson had a great distaste for the spiritistic point of view and method of approach to the mysteries of life and death. He returns to this again and again in his letters:

One asks where and when will this sloppy thing stop! I have recently seen a printed communication from W. T. Stead, the spirit, on Madame Blavatsky, through a medium in Australia. They give an added horror to death! I frankly prefer old church Christianity, even with its limitations.

Of Grierson's marvellous musical gift I am not competent to speak, because I never heard him perform and I know nothing about music anyway. His was solely and utterly an art of *improvisation*, and it appears always to have produced upon the auditors a wonderful effect, deep in proportion to their musical sensitivity. Those who knew most about music were loudest in their praises. I have the assurance of Arthur Farwell, a composer and orchestra leader of the first order, that Grierson's gift of improvisation, and the strange and moving character of the music were inexplicable, and unique in his experience. Because our mutual absorptions were occult and literary Grierson has little to say, in his letters to me, about musical matters. This is the only reference I find:

The truth is, my finest music is *esoteric!* And more so today than ever before. How can the big public understand? It is impossible. How am I to explain to a dense public fed up on rag-time? How is one to make them see the difference between a spiritual and esoteric *improvisation* and music played from notes from a cold-blooded, reasoned, and so-called classical mode? There is nothing so false in art today, as our music. Busoni, the great pianist, is right when he declares that improvisation is like a portrait from life, written music like a model. It is the difference between life and dead form. All this must be preached and taught fearlessly, but I cannot attempt it until I obtain material independence. I must keep my mouth closed until the day of deliverance.

That day, alas, never came, and the only deliverance for this gallant spirit was death. Prophet, philosopher, poet, musician, he reminds me, as I said in the beginning, of Rostand's Cyrano de Bergerac, particularly in his lifelong frustration, and in the tragic circumstance of his death:

> He flew high and fell back again
> A pretty wit — whose like we lack —
> A lover . . . not like other men . . .
> .   .   .   .
> Who was all things — and all in vain.

For truly he seems already strangely forgotten: his music, never recorded, is only a memory in the minds of those who heard it; his books — little masterpieces of thought and expression — are out of print and unobtainable even in most libraries; in touch, at one time or another, with most of the eminent people of his time

[158]

he had the misfortune to outlive them, and the friends who survived him seem to be now so few that the candles on that altar which show him to be still remembered appear to be all snuffed out saving, perhaps, this single one.

THE WORLD OF THE WONDROUS

XVIII

FAERY LORE

(Dora Van Gelder)

READER, are you one of those with soul so dead that you do not believe in fairies — one who didn't respond to Peter Pan's appeal for Tinker Bell? Or perhaps you imagine that modern science, which has " electrocuted Santa Claus " has made such a belief impossible. Then you are not up on modern science. A. S. Eddington, one of its high priests, in his The Nature of the Physical World has nothing to say about fairies — naturally — but he has something to say about that segment of life in which, if they exist, we might expect to find them, a demesne which science is forced to recognize but is powerless to explore. " Certain states of awareness in consciousness " he says, " have at least equal significance with those which are called sensations . . . amid these must be found the basis of experience from which a spiritual religion arises " — and, let it be added, faery lore. Science, in becoming more profound, has assumed an attitude less arrogant, and now avowedly deals only with what Eddington calls " the metrical world," the one with which our senses and our reasoning faculty are able to establish relations. We used to call this the " real " world, but now we know better, so Eddington calls it " the world of concreteness." Matter has been dissolved into energy and energy into motion, but what is it that moves? Science cannot answer. Though it is neither " mind " nor " stuff " the best name that Eddington can find for it is mind-stuff, because it is alone apprehensible by the mind, and one with its nature.

Now mind implies consciousness, and consciousness, so far as our experience extends, is an attribute of a person or a being — a condition of beingness, at all events. Therefore that vast sector of life out of which science reserves for itself one little segment — the part which can be measured — we are free to conceive of as peopled with beings: thrones, dominions, principalities, powers, cherubim and seraphim — fairies too, if we prefer, and science will not have power to say us nay.

But my purpose is not to convince you of the existence of fairies but to introduce you to Dora Van Gelder. If you knew her she would herself go far toward convincing you, for she is the most fairy-like being, not only in her looks and gestures, but psychologically — only I suppose I should not use that word, since fairies are popularly believed to have no souls. Perhaps, like Hans Andersen's little Sea Maiden, she came to earth to get one, for Dora seems a creature self-exiled from her native element, and though obliged " in this harsh world to draw her breath in pain " she follows our folk-ways

With much love
Dora

Dora Van Gelder

in no martyr's spirit, but gallantly, joyously. Beset by so much to which, by reason of our coarser fibre, we are immune, she is free, on the other hand, of many of our emotional complexes, and awake to worlds of which we are totally unaware. Although she is not small enough to nestle in a nutshell or swing upon a cobweb, judged by human standards Dora is diminutive and slender — all " fire and dew," with a faun-like face, and a fawn-like swiftness and gracefulness of gesture. Her clairvoyance — I call it that, though if you are a skeptic you may call it her vivid imagination if you prefer — she inherits not only from her parents, but from her grandparents, all of whom possessed " second sight." Added to this, she was educated by Mr. C. W. Leadbeater, who is perhaps the greatest living clairvoyant. Her extraordinary faculty therefore seemed to herself the most natural thing in the world, and it was with surprise and something of a shock that she woke up to the fact that she was looked upon as a unique and somewhat freakish person.

The first thing that I tried to get from Dora was some idea of the relation of the world of faery and the world of mortals. She did her best to enlighten me, but I shall have to formulate what I gathered in language very different from her own. Generally speaking the faery world is related to the world we know as soul to body, for it represents the life side of nature, and the physical world the form side, though the faery world has its forms, just as the physical world has its life-forces. But in the faery world forms are more subtle, ethereal, fluidic, the life-forces flow less sluggishly, as against a diminished resistance. In that world the spirit builds the house, in this, the house confines the spirit. The two worlds are the reciprocals of one another, their interrelation, interpenetration and interaction is continuous and complete. They are, indeed, one world, their differentiation from one another in our consciousness being due to the trifling but to us all-important fact that there are certain wavelengths which awaken responses in our sensory mechanism to which we give the names of sound, color and form, and therefore we are able to think of certain things as " real " and their totality as the real world; whereas with the other octaves of vibration we are unable to establish such relation, and the producing causes of these vibrations have for us therefore no reality — do not seem to exist at all, yet the difference is only one of vibratory rate. To illustrate what I mean, there are few things which appear more real and substantial, for example, than the brass propellors of an electric fan when they are at rest; but turn on the current and set these metal wings in motion, and they become more and more diaphanous until they disappear and one can actually see through them — only our memory and perhaps the stir of the air in the room, assures us that they are there. This world beyond the world is already a commonplace of science, and even the man on the street

[166]

is reconciled to ideas which his common sense finds it difficult to deal with — invisible light, soundless sounds and formless forms.

The function of fairies, Dora tells me, is to transform and direct the solar energy into its appropriate channels and to supervise, guide and stimulate its action. They are the receivers and administrators of the life-force, much in the same sense that bankers, brokers and business men are the receivers and administrators of the flow of gold. Broadly speaking, fairies, or nature spirits, (if one prefers so to call them), belong to four different categories, those of the air, of fire, of water and of earth. This corresponds to the familiar mediaeval classification into sylphs, salamanders, undines and gnomes. The earth and water fairies are much nearer to us than those of air and fire, so near, in fact, that it is not difficult to establish relations with them, for they are curious about us, and inclined to be friendly, particularly with children, whose " invisible playmates " they often become. Psychologically they have much in common with the higher animals, but are more intelligent, particularly as regards their work, in which they take great interest and pride. They have no general ideas, however, and small power of concentration, and when not engaged in directing and assisting the processes of vegetation they spend their time in play. They are subject to and under the direction of *devas*, or angels, a higher order of being altogether, to whom they stand in something the same relation that domestic animals stand to man, though their servitude is voluntary, and their attitude toward their masters is one of reverence.

The garden fairies help the flowers and shrubs to unfold and grow according to their archetypal pattern; they are small, and their faces and forms approximate the human, though often in a distorted or exaggerated kind of way. They have no wings, and are of various colors — indeed, Dora says that all fairies traverse space without the aid of wings. Water fairies are of two kinds, those which she calls " water babies," on account of their diminutive and globular appearance, which preside over the life of the surface and of the shallows, and the deep-sea fairies, which are more like demons: large, terrifying, and inimical to man. The fire fairies are likewise to man indifferent or hostile, delighting in destruction, hurrying to augment great conflagrations much as firemen hurry to put them out. Household and hearth fires are fed by fairies of the salamander type, small and short-lived. Air fairies are of all the most beautiful and beneficent: Dora says that many so-called " guardian angels " are simply air fairies who are friendly to man.

Fairies vary in different parts of the world, and under varying conditions, just as human beings do. In the National Yellowstone Park, Dora encountered a unique order of fairies seeming to have something in common with the North American Indian. The tree-spirits of the giant sequoias are far greater, older and more intelligent according to her notion, than any man. Their sense of time is different from ours, they do not grow old, nor were they ever young, a thousand years ago are as yesterday, and they watch the procession of the generations of man as we watch the waves on the sand. When the tree which these spirits ensoul is felled or otherwise destroyed they die with it, but death wears to them a different face, being merely a painless dissolution into the universal reservoir of life. The greatest *deva* Dora says she ever encountered is the *genius loci* of the Grand Canyon of the Colorado, which pervades, according to her, the entire place and can be felt even by those not gifted with her sixth sense.

I asked Dora how she communicated with her fairy friends and she explained that it was by means of mental images: she drew pictures in her imagination of the things she wanted to communicate and these they seemed able to apprehend, and answered in similar fashion. With the more intelligent fairies and with the *devas*, however, communication is telepathic, and therefore direct. Dora once asked one of her fairy friends who inhabited a public park in Australia, his idea of a human being, and he drew a picture of a fat woman with a basket, littering the lawns, breaking the branches and treading down the flowers! She described another amusing encounter with a little brown fellow in Central Park, where she had gone with a New York newspaper reporter in search for fairies to tell about in the public press. It was in early spring, and the brownie was busily engaged stimulating the run of sap in a bush, and didn't want to be interrupted, but finally consented to an interview. Dora had the greatest difficulty in making him understand that she wanted to put him in the papers, because the only function a newspaper had, according to his experience, was to litter up the grass!

I asked Dora if fairies were differentiated sexually and she said that they were not, in the sense that human beings are, but they are nevertheless of two kinds, active and passive, positive and negative, the primal differentiation of which physical sex is the expression. She seemed unclear as to how their bodies were created, but it was by no process of physical generation and gestation, but rather by some image-making faculty through an intention of consciousness — some precipitation from the thought world to the world of form.

The world of faery appears to be like that of Eden before the fall, before free-will and the knowledge of good and evil had disturbed the universal harmony: it is a joyous, harmonious world, full of light, color and music in which is no suffering, no sin, no frustration and no death, things which the fairies do not appear to understand.

XIX

A FOOTNOTE ON Æ

(George W. Russell)

My contacts with Æ have not been such as would entitle me to write about him, save for the fact that on the one occasion when we really met, he so revealed himself — not, I hasten to add, through any power of mine to precipitate confidences, but because he is one of those rare persons who are great enough and simple enough to *live openly*. Everything he does is self-revelatory: his paintings are the report of his clairvoyance; his poems are records of his flashes of insight, deep memories and cosmic dreams; in his critical and editorial writing the workings of his mind may be seen as through a glass, but not " darkly "; and his lectures are reveries which he permits his auditors to share.

My early contacts with Æ were nebulous and indirect; a mutual friend, a beautiful Irishwoman living in Toronto, had among her prized possessions a drawing of a *deva* which Æ had given her, the graphic record of a thing seen, not imagined, he had said. The face was like that of a Burne-Jones angel, but less anæmic — the androgynous type; the head was covered with a growth of strange, flamboyant feathers, sweeping backward from the forehead like the tail of a comet; no wings were visible, for wings are made to beat the air with, and therefore things of this three-dimensional section of the world. Later, I found two more of his paintings in the house of another friend in Buffalo, New York, and again I seemed to draw near to a nature which had known moments of vision of an intensity sufficient to make report of them after this fashion —

> For he on honeydew hath fed
> And sipped the milk of paradise.

Along with several hundred others, I saw the man himself for the first time at the Poetry Society's dinner in his honor: a large, shaggy man who beamed beneficently through his spectacles — it was not difficult to believe that he is the most loved man in Ireland, as we were assured by each of the speakers in turn. Even Ernest Boyd, the super-cynic, who introduced him, purred happily on this occasion, putting his claws out only once, and then in playfulness. This was when he accused Æ — who abhors cynicism — of being the author of the supremely cynical remark that the Irish literary movement was made up, for the most part, of men who hated one another. Æ's speech proved a delight to those who were near enough to hear it; the effect was of a low-voiced, but exquisitely uttered reverie embroidered with that witty and rich imagery which is

[172]

(Photograph copyrighted by Pirie MacDonald)

George W. Russell, " Æ "

Erin's gift to her poet-sons — "Yeats always lights his cigarettes from the stars" is an example of this delightful quality.

After the ritual of the dinner had run its course we were introduced to one another, but under the circumstances this amounted to no more than shaking hands with the President at a White House reception, for the crowd was large, and the confusion correspondingly great. A few days later, however, through the kindness of a woman friend, I was enabled to meet Æ under conditions favorable to conversation, and we talked of "matters of great pith and moment" pertaining to the inner life.

The thing which impressed me first about him was a certain fine modesty which took the form of self-depreciation. To praise of his pictures he replied, "But I never learned to draw properly, I had no right instruction," and to praise of his lectures, "I'm not used to these big audiences, it seems I don't make myself heard." The second thing which struck me was his rare simplicity of manner; among the six or seven people gathered that afternoon to do him honor, he was acquainted with only one — or at most two — but he treated us all as though he had known us always, and the talk was intimate, as it is among friends.

Of what he told us I shall here repeat only so much as I believe he would not mind my sharing. One story, aside from its intrinsic interest, gives a hint of the possible derivation of his pseudonym, Æ. He said that when he was a boy he was just like other boys, was interested in the same things, and read the same boys' stories, except that he seemed to have a more vivid imagination, for he was always telling himself wonderful stories of gods and demi-gods, and miraculous happenings in some Valhalla, and to these characters he assigned names. He had no other idea but that he invented these stories and these names. But one day while waiting at the desk of the village library for the librarian to bring him a story book, he happened to glance at the open page of a book that was lying there, and his eye encountered the word " Aeon." He declared that his surprise and excitement were so great that he left the library empty-handed and walked about the streets for two hours before he could muster up sufficient calmness and courage to ask the librarian what book it was, and if he might look at it. For the name Aeon was one which he had given to the hero of one of his own stories, a name which he regarded as peculiarly his own, or of his own invention, and it was upsetting to discover that such was plainly not the case. The book proved to be a treatise on Gnostic religion and cosmogony and in it, to his utter amazement, he found recorded, in a mass of legendary lore, those very stories which he thought he had invented — even the names of the characters were the same. This forced him to the conclusion that either his imaginings were recovered memories of things learned or experienced in some antecedent life, or that in some inexplicable manner he had tapped, so to speak, the memory of nature — turned over the leaves of some invisible fourth-dimensional photograph album containing pictures of the past, or thoughts about the past. In The Candle of Vision Æ refers to the above narrated experience in the following words, " I have glanced in passing at a book left open by some one in a library and the words first seen thrilled me, for they confirmed a knowledge lately attained in vision."

The Gaelic renaissance, he informed us, was the outgrowth of the theosophical movement in Ireland in that its prime movers were most of them theosophists. This is implicit also in William Butler Yeats' reminiscences, himself a pupil of Madame Blavatsky, and a dabbler in occult arts. Æ told us of that strange household in Dublin to which Yeats refers, the chief interest of whose members was the study of theosophy, the practice of ritualistic magic, and the development of the higher powers of the self. Though they all had their living to earn, according to Æ they devoted their spare time with great ardor to these pursuits. Their studies and experiments were directed and aided by a mysterious teacher, adept in these arts, though he was forced to leave Ireland, for political reasons, after a sojourn of less than a year.

Æ declared that extraordinary results were sometimes obtained by group meditation under this teacher, and that with his aid some of them were enabled to recover scenes and episodes from some long vanished period of time in which it appeared they had been together — as celebrants of ancient religious rites. They were able to see the streets of some old city, and a stone-lined chamber, entered through a metal door. Not all of them were thus clairvoyant; some merely sensed what was going on, as the blind sense things, while others had only *moments* of vision. The success of the results of group meditation was conditioned by the degree of harmony prevailing among the members, and this harmony was the most difficult thing to achieve and maintain, for in sex some were antipodal and all were Irish!

Æ told of a strange thing which happened to him once in connection with his painting; he had a great admiration of the landscapes of Corot, and wanted mightily to know by what technical process he achieved the soft lambency of his grey and turquoise skies. While standing one day in front of one of Corot's canvases filled with such thoughts and such desires, the picture seemed slowly to expand before his eyes, in both dimensions, with the effect that every brush-stroke, the very texture of the canvas itself, became visible as under a microscope, revealing to him Corot's painting method as no description could. The next morning, Æ affirms, he painted a Corot quite in the Corot manner, far more successfully than he could otherwise have done.

Æ expressed himself as much pleased with America

and the Americans he had met, although the social wave so overwhelmed him that for the first time in his life he failed to remember everyone. The skyscrapers of course amazed him, and it was difficult for him to comprehend the power which sent these giant growths skyward, and created the torrent of life which flowed through the canyons at their base. It seemed to him that if he could sit quietly down in the midst of this hurly-burly in presence of these monsters of the market, and meditate upon them, some revelation might perhaps be vouchsafed; but this was a desire the gratification of which, from considerations of mere safety, he found it necessary to deny himself. The picture has often haunted my imagination of this great bearded, burly, yet curiously child-like man seated, at the rush hour, on the curb where Fifth Avenue crosses Forty Second Street, oblivious of everyone, intent only upon those cloud-piercing steel and stone Valhallas, searching his inner consciousness for their Word of Power.

The justification of this so personal a memoir of Æ I cull from something he himself has written, for in The Candle of Vision he says: " If I tell what I know, and how I came to see most clearly, I may give hope to those who would fain believe in that world the seers spake of, but who cannot understand the language written by those who had seen that beauty of old, or who may have thought the ancient scriptures but a record of extravagant desires."

THE BLACK LACQUER CHEST

THIS is a ghost's story — as faint and evanescent as breath on a window pane; and — to carry out the figure — that pane was the consciousness of a woman through which shone at times a light that never was on sea or land, a pane upon which appeared strange images etched there by some lightning science knows not of. This is just one of those images, the most amazing, sweet, sad, wistful of them all.

My wife was a psychic. I loathe the word with all its shifty, shabby connotations, and she hated it as much as I; but her psychism is part of the story, the plate, as it were, on which the image was imprinted, therefore I must begin with that. How shall I describe this faculty, as much a part of her as her olive pallor or her crow-black hair? Like Socrates, who had his *dæmon* she felt that she too had a familiar spirit, angel, guide, philosopher and friend; I know not how to name it or describe it, but she called it her oracle. To her it was in a sense both master and servant, for on her part she obeyed it implicitly, and in return it told her anything she wanted to know or understand — where to go, what to do, where

[178]

lost things were hidden, what absent friends were doing at the moment, the sort of person So-and-so might be, what would follow from this or that. It unlocked the door to the past, it even raised the curtain on the future and in all the seven years my bird-wife and I lived together I do not recall a single instance in which her oracle played her false.

The method of communication was by automatic writing, and in a script entirely different from her ordinary hand. They lie before me as I write, the documents in the case of the Black Lacquer Chest, as I might call them, a scant sheaf of sandal-wood-scented papers already faintly yellowed at the edges although the writing is scarcely twelve years old. There are the familiar delicate round back-hand of the messages proper and the angular inclined script of her own annotations giving the subject and the date. April twenty-nine, nineteen hundred and sixteen is the earliest. At that time we were living in the outskirts of Rochester, New York, in a bird-haunted park, the last little remnant of a forest primeval which had miraculously escaped the woodman's axe. From that high eyrie we were wont to descend upon the city on business or on pleasure bent. One of the favorite haunts of our leisure was a little shop kept by two women, where could be purchased at reasonable prices the products and spoils of far-away " heathen " lands, supplied for the most part by Christian missionaries who eked out their scant incomes by these means.

It was there that we discovered the black lacquer chest. The shop-owners had bought it in a neighboring town, where it had lain for seventy-five years at least, in the attic of one of the old houses. It had been brought to this country by a seaman and given to his mother. He told her that it was worth enough money to pay all her debts. It was sold at auction, after her death.

It was an oblong box of a size and weight not too great to be easily lifted by a lady into her lap, the outside bearing intricate designs, containing figures, all in gold, the base and cornice richly decorated, and the whole supported on four small carved feet. Clearly it was a woman's workbox, for inside was a tray full of odd shaped implements for sewing and embroidering exquisitely carved in ivory, and along with these, in incongruous juxtaposition, was a mother-of-pearl crucifix — Spanish, sixteenth century, I should say at a guess. With this exception, the chest and everything in it appeared to be of Chinese design and workmanship, one of those little masterpieces of inspired craftsmanship of the sort to excite the cupidity of collectors — a museum piece in point of fact.

My wife was fascinated with this beautiful object, so redolent of the perfume of the East and of the past, but the price asked, though far below the real value, was prohibitive so far as we were concerned, and we relinquished the hope of possessing it ourselves. It so happened however that a rich bachelor, a dear friend of us both, having searched vainly in the New York shops for a present for a bride at whose wedding he was to be the groom's best man, asked our advice and help. We immediately suggested the black lacquer chest. He was charmed with the idea, and with the thing itself. It passed, in this way, out of our ken — all save the Spanish crucifix, which we accepted as a gift from our friend.

But in the interval between the discovery of the chest and its final disposition we obtained with the aid of the oracle what I suppose would be called its " psychometric record," and this, exactly, is my story — shadowy, slight, inconclusive as a story, but perhaps a thread connecting past and present, this world and some other, like a cobweb across a crevasse.

The first thing my wife did, after she had seen the chest, was to ask her oracle about it, and this is what her hand wrote down:

" *Eugenie, the box contained the belongings of a person to whom you were deeply attached, and it has come again into your life as a link by which the spirit of the past may hold you to the path you trod then, and which alone can lead you to the light.*"

Then something happened entirely foreign to all our experience with the oracle: this " person," in the midst of the next message, assumes the rôle of protagonist and tells her own story.

[181]

" Zanner was her name: a beautiful child, a woman lost in a land of strangers, she longed with the deep despair of the children of men for the home of her fathers.

" Let your thoughts follow full carefully that you confuse not my meaning. The box was the gift of my father to me on the day we celebrate as birthday, for it is when the age of womanhood is opening. It held the forms of my youth so sweet in their innocence. And then they dragged me away and sold me, the beautiful daughter of Humas. Full Hindu I was, but the gift of my father was the artist's work of another land. Men of great skill came to us. It was made full three hundred and more years ago. It was stolen from my home in the land of the Samurai."

This sent us to a more careful examination of the chest, and we found that the decorations consisted of representations of a family life amid refined surroundings — what might very well have been the artist's idea of a birthday party, in point of fact. The workmanship was evidently Chinese, but the scenery, people and costumes were not characteristic of that country. We were confused, too, by the reference to " the land of the Samurai," and asked for further enlightenment. As before, the oracle speaks first, and then the girl herself takes up the tale:

" The box will reveal itself. You confused our mean-

*ing. She was a full Hindu in the land of the Samurai.
Her father was there to represent. . . .*

"*The box was made in India by a Chinese artist. My
father went as a royal messenger to Japan. Full some
years we dwelt there because a great fear was upon my
father to return; fear for his life was of his brother, who
hated my father. Humas was the son of a prince high
in power. In that land I was very happy, but afterwards
my father was killed and I was stolen away and sold to
a prince of India, who treated me as a woman condemned. The time of my death is recorded in the land of
my birth, for I was great, and even in my fallen state I
was remembered. Houmas was the name of my father.
Full of memories sweet and sad I suffered long im-
prisonment, and it was stolen by strangers from another
land. Fear full terrible I knew.*"

The concluding message is in the nature of a lament,
casting upon the darkness of our ignorance a final lurid
gleam, and constituting a plea for peace on earth on
entirely novel grounds; for at the time this message was
received the World War was still in progress.

"*It is pain to think in form of words. If the earth were
at peace my soul could rest, but I suffer for the pain of
the struggling souls that surround me.*"

Thereafter, upon the subject of this mystery, the
oracle was mute, but it had this to tell us about the
mother-of-pearl crucifix:

" The crucifix is one that was given to a man known in the East as a great follower of the light that shines within, for he held great power over the Christian Chinese. He was of the country, but became, at great sacrifice, a priest of the church."

These constitute " the documents in the case." Are they of any evidential value? That is to say, is this a gleam lighting up some " dark backward and abysm of time," having reference to actual events and real personages, or are these merely the vaporings of some subliminal self, set in motion by memory or suggestion, as unfounded and irresponsible as those dreams which arise as a result of the dramatic sundering of the ego during sleep? I can offer no certain evidence of the truth of the former hypothesis, though such evidence may somewhere exist. But Zanner's story fits fairly well into the place and period to which she has assigned it. " Full three hundred and more years ago " in the history of India takes us into the reign of the Mogul emperors, where in 1530 Humaioun (Humaious, Humayun, Huma, Umar, according to different spellings) succeeded to the throne of Baber. Here was a prince who spent his life in agitation or in exile, by reason of his fear of Karman his brother, and he is known to have had, by various wives, a number of daughters, but there is no record of his having gone to Japan, Persia having been the place of his ten-year exile.

And so my story must end with a question mark, and on a rising inflection. This may disappoint the literal minded, and those seeking evidence of the persistence of consciousness beyond the grave. But to me, and I hope to some who may read this, Zanner's story lives like a sweet, sad strain of music, haunting the memory, because " it hath a dying fall." Out of the so-called subconscious she flashes forth like a silver fish momentarily hooked from out some deep river — she is beautiful, she suffers, she is gone.

XXI

TOLD BY THE TEA SALESMAN

In that same Far East Shop where I discovered the black lacquer chest I one day encountered a handsome young Hindu who represented himself as a tea salesman, and who certainly had many interesting things to say about that marvellous medicinal eastern herb. Like all the other orientals I had ever met he did not fail to discover, underneath the veneer of my occidental culture and my Anglo-Saxon mask, my essential kinship with his continent of thought and feeling, and accordingly in our brief interview we got on excellently well.

My wife and I were given to late hours, and one night after midnight, while we were sitting before the dying fire, a knock came at the front door. Our house was situated in the midst of what was once a large private estate, adjoining Mount Hope cemetery, a locality little frequented. Visitors were rare with us at any hour, and at such an hour quite unprecedented. The knock fell on our ears, therefore, with something of the sinister effect of the " knocking within " upon the ears of Macbeth and his spouse, and as I went to open the door my curiosity was not unmixed with apprehension.

[186]

This proved groundless, however, for there, to my surprise, stood the Tea Salesman. He proceeded to explain that by reason of the noise and promiscuity of the city at all hours of the day and night, the only inviolate place in which he found it possible to pursue those meditations which had become a habit of his life was the city cemetery after the gates were closed for the night. He had just come from these devotions, and knowing that we lived near by, he had found his way to our door, guided by our late-lighted window. We made him welcome, and he stayed and talked for several hours. The visit was repeated once or twice thereafter. Certain things he told us and showed us I have never forgotten: these I shall record.

He was born and brought up in the foothills of the Himalayas, in a society so remote from the fret of the tide of all that goes by the name of civilization as to retain its primitive, patriarchal character almost completely unimpaired. Like most of the Hindus I have encountered, he regarded the British occupancy of India in the light of a misfortune, and claimed that his countrymen had been happier, healthier, better educated and better fed before the Anglo-Saxon invasion than they had been since. He averred that the British had exported wheat in large quantities in times of famine; that they had disrupted the ancient native school system and given nothing in its place; they had destroyed handicraft and household arts in favor of factory production; and by

their lust for slaughter they had antagonized and ter-
rorized the animal world to such an extent that the
number of deaths from tigers, cobras and other animals
and reptiles was greater and not less than formerly. He
declared that before the invasion of the armed and
helmeted hunters wild animals had no hostility to man,
because they had no fear of him: they recognized him as
superior, but friendly. He declared that in the old
days, when prowling tigers threatened the sheepfold, his
grandfather used to go and drive them away with the
branch of a tree, as one might a cat or a dog, and that
they submitted to such treatment — slunk away, so to
speak, with their tails between their legs, cowed by a
will superior to theirs.

But all this, whether true or false — and we knew not
which — interested us less than his accounts of his spiritual teacher, and certain things which he had said. For,
following the ancient custom, our friend had lived for
a time in the *ashrama* of his master, doing menial service in exchange for instruction in the " secret doctrine "
and those disciplines necessary for the acquisition of
powers whereby precept is proven by practice, counsel
is transmuted into conduct of life.

This teacher must have been an altogether extraordinary person. I once asked Paul Richard, who for ten
years travelled up and down the world searching for
wisdom, whom he considered to be the wisest and most
spiritually developed men he had ever met. Without any

hesitation he answered that in India he had encountered certain holy men who seemed to him to represent the very summit of human evolution, mental and spiritual, and that none of the contemporary so-called great men of our European world were at all in their class. The Tea Salesman made the same high claim for his teacher; he felt that merely to have lived under the same roof with such a man for a period of years was fortune's most munificent gift, one by which he was more ennobled than by the highest honor the world had in its power to bestow.

According to him, his teacher's vision of human life and human destiny embraced cycles of time and dimensions of space immeasurably greater than the brief span of years and the limited space-frame of the personal self. He appeared to have knowledge not only of the past, but of the future, and accurately forecast certain crises in the life of his pupil, and forewarned him of them. " You will leave India," he had told him, " and go to that land where people of all nations are being flung, as into a crucible, in order to produce that new race which will inaugurate an altogether new civilization and culture, and bring about a renewal of the spiritual forces always latent in mankind. The seed of this awakening must come, as it has always come, from Mother India, but the soil in which that seed will germinate will be fertilized by western science, which all unknowingly is approaching the eastern wisdom because the watchword of the high priests of that science, is identical with our own: *There is no religion higher than Truth.* For many lives your destiny has been preparing you to be a sower of this spiritual seed, but you will sow it in sorrow, poverty and bitterness, because you will not be able, in this life, to rid yourself of the evil karma accumulated in former lives."

This prophecy was then in process of fulfillment, for the young man acknowledged frankly that he had always to struggle against a perverse and passionate nature, destroying, at one stroke, the fruitage of laborious, well-spent days, and making it necessary to begin all over again. He never confessed these derelictions to his master, because they were known to him as soon as they were committed, and sometimes apparently even before. But he said that though contrite, he was never ashamed in the presence of his master, because though the circumstances were known to him to the last detail and in all their enormity, he also knew the ancient and hard-tied knot in the tangled skein of his pupil's destiny — every thought of his mind and desire of his heart — given which, the dénouement could not have been other than it was, at that period of his unfoldment, and therefore by this all-discerning and compassionate intelligence could not but be forgiven.

The toleration of this teacher was proportionate to his insight: he affirmed that the most frightful and degraded human conditions and predicaments have a compensatory value — not for the superficial self, perhaps, but for the true self — the ego. In its longer lifetime of which each earthly incarnation is as but a day, a single life as a criminal or as a courtesan is not without its value, for the reason that the first qualification for entering " the path " is *discrimination*, and these adversaries and sacrificial victims of organized society are in a position to see humanity without its moralistic mask: to them the people they encounter appear, not as they wish the world to believe them, but " just as they really are " — stripped, by their passions, of their own pretense.

I had always been curious to learn the truth about eastern magic, concerning which there are so many conflicting stories told, some claiming that from top to bottom it is all mere legerdemain, while others hold that in its higher and more rarely witnessed manifestations it involves a control over the human mind, or over the forces of nature — or both — to which no occidental magician has ever attained. The Tea Salesman, pressed on this point, affirmed the latter view; questioned further, he admitted that he had himself acquired from his master a certain expertness in this direction, but on the understanding that it should never be used nor displayed save in the furtherance of some altruistic end. Whereupon I asked him if he would not consent to give some demonstration, then and there, which would set my mind forever at rest upon this debated point. I had myself been a student and practitioner of legerdemain for a period of years, and had read most of the literature upon the subject: I felt confident, therefore, of being able to detect to which order of deception I was being subjected.

Thus challenged, the Tea Salesman consented to put the matter to the test, though only after exacting the promise that we would never betray him to another Hindu whom we knew in common, who also possessed these powers, we were informed, but thought it wrong to display them under any circumstances. My wife and I were both, I may say, in a skeptical frame of mind: the thing had resolved itself into a duel of wits between two opposite and largely antagonistic cultures, and both personally and in our representative capacity we had no wish to lose.

The first thing he did was to take a large, black-covered book which happened to be lying on the table, and place it under the lamp in a position where it would catch the light, leaving it there for several minutes. Then he took it in his hand and knelt down on the rug in front of the sofa where we were sitting. Next he asked me if I had a silver coin which I would let him take for the experiment. I handed him a silver half-dollar, first taking pains to nick the edge of it with my knife. My mind travelled with lightning-like rapidity to every coin trick I had ever seen or heard of — I had known Nelson Downs, " King of the Koins " — and I took pains to assure myself that there was no horse-hair attached to the coat sleeve or to the vest button, with a bit of wax on the free end. He engaged in no slightest manipulation, no misdirection, but simply laid the coin I had handed him near the lower edge of the black book, held at a slight angle. We were told to watch it intently, for presently it would begin to move. All this time he was still kneeling immediately in front of us, so near that we could have touched him; with his right hand he held the book in position, his disengaged left hand hung at his side. The room was sufficiently though not abundantly lighted; I never felt more alert, more alive, in fuller possession of all my faculties.

We watched; nothing happened; I felt that western skepticism had conquered; on my wife's face, also, which was within the field of my vision, I fancied I could detect the dawning of an ironic, slightly triumphant smile, when lo! to our amazement, the coin *did* begin to move, sliding slowly up the book-cover, onto the hand, then the arm of the Tea Salesman, until it reached the elbow; when it climbed up the sleeve of his upper arm, reached the shoulder, from whence it was plucked by his free left hand, and given without a moment's delay or a superfluous gesture directly into my hand. I could still feel the spur made by my knife. I looked and felt for some sign of wax but there was none. I was completely baffled; I had no idea how the trick was done.

The Tea Salesman explained — though what he meant

by it I have not the least idea — that the illusion was part physical and part metaphysical; that it involved a higher power of hypnotism, unknown in the West, because attainable only by continued and intense concentration. By these means he had imposed his own mental image upon our minds and senses. He declared that in reality the coin had never left his hand. I believed him then, and I believe still, that this is the true explanation, though the one for which I was the least prepared, because no one had ever succeeded in hypnotizing me in any degree or manner up to that time.

There is a certain amount of reliable testimony that this higher power of hypnotism exists. There is the story of the trick Madame Blavatsky — an adept in these arts, having been trained, like the Tea Salesman in the *ashrama* of a master — played upon a young man belonging to the travelling party to which she also was attached. He was fond of sketching, and was always asking the others to suggest subjects. One day while they were picnicking beside a lake, Madame Blavatsky set him to sketching an island which was not there at all, she having impressed the image of it upon his consciousness so powerfully as to create the illusion of reality. The others, who were in the secret, were much amused to see him hard at work on such a task. As a climax, she withdrew him from his illusion, much to his bewilderment and chagrin. Professor Max Heinsholdt, while travelling in India, tells of witnessing the familiar mango trick performed by a holy man in a manner entirely different from the way in which the ordinary street fakirs performed it. Instead of producing, from a seed planted in the ground, a little shoot a few inches high, a towering tree grew up, remained during the period of his discourse, and then gradually dissolved. The interesting fact is, that Heinsholdt, who was of a scientific and enquiring turn of mind, moved from his original position, going first toward the tree and then away from it; and in each case, as he did so, the image grew indistinct and disappeared, only to reappear when he resumed his first position. He noted also that two English officers, who had come up after the crowd was gathered and the trick underway, evidently saw nothing of it, and were much puzzled to know what everyone was gazing at. The professor took a kodak of the tree, but the developed negative showed nothing, all of which indicates, I think, that the Tea Salesman told us the truth.

Such things are certainly less difficult to believe than formerly, for the line between physics and metaphysics is shifting and uncertain. When a scientist of the eminence of Eddington can find no better name for the constitution of the universe and the background of phenomenality than " mind stuff " there can be nothing preposterous in the idea of communicable mental images.

The Tea Salesman ceased his visits without warning, vanishing out of our lives as mysteriously as he had entered. I have often wondered what has become of him: I picture him as still selling his excellent teas. I wish for him better places for meditation than among the graves of the dead, and I hope that he is fulfilling his destiny by scattering seeds of that wisdom learned among those sacred mountains from that holy man.

XXII

THE ROMANCE AND MYSTERY OF
"TERTIUM ORGANUM"

IN the spring of 1918 there appeared at my door a young Russian, Nicholas Bessaraboff, bearing in his hand the Russian edition of Tertium Organum. He had determined that the book must be translated into English, and, since his knowledge of the language was inadequate for the task, he asked my help. To this I readily agreed, and we set to work almost immediately. Our method was this: he made a word-for-word translation of the Russian text, and when I had the meaning clear in my mind I expressed it in the best and simplest English I could command.

I had had some experience as a publisher, having issued my own books and others under my own imprint, and I therefore decided to follow the same procedure with Tertium Organum, as by these means I could keep more intimately in touch with those who bought and read the book.

Meantime, we knew nothing of Ouspensky, his whereabouts, or whether he were alive or dead. We made an effort to trace him through Washington and through the

Red Cross, but by reason of Russia being cut off from the rest of the world these attempts failed. Our first hint of his whereabouts came through some letters he contributed to The New Age, an English review, discovered and called to our attention by Dhan Gopal Mukerji, the Hindu dramatist. In answer to our appeal for information, A. R. Orage, the then editor of The New Age, informed us that though he knew Ouspensky, and had been in correspondence with him, he had left southern Russia for parts unknown.

It was through Spencer Kellogg, Jr., of Buffalc, that we finally obtained definite news of Ouspensky. Being in England during the summer of 1920, he dropped in at the headquarters of the Theosophical Society to enquire if they had Tertium Organum on sale. There he encountered a Russian woman who proved to be Ouspensky's friend, and knew his address. He and his family were refugees in Constantinople; having lost everything in the Revolution, they were in need, and Ouspensky was anxious to come to England, where he had friends, and would be able to support himself by his pen.

On receipt of this news Bessaraboff wrote Ouspensky a letter, telling him the story of the translation and publication of Tertium Organum, and I sent him two copies of the book and a substantial money payment, representing accrued author's royalties. In due course Bessaraboff received an answer, of which the following is a part:

[198]

" TERTIUM ORGANUM "

Constantinople, 11/17/20.

MY DEAR NICHOLAY ALEXANDROVITCH:

I received your letter of September 24, together with a parcel and letter from Mr. Bragdon. First of all let me thank you and Mr. Bragdon for the excellent translation and remarkably elegant edition of my book. It is of course very pleasant for any author to see his book in such an edition, and " T. O." is to a certain extent my weakness, although now I should change many things there. This I hope to do in the next edition.*

Certainly I cannot but feel that you and Mr. Bragdon are my friends, especially because Mr. Bragdon's book [Four-Dimensional Vistas] startled me by its nearness to " T. O." There is only one other book in which I have also found much similarity to my own thought: this is The Science of Peace, by Bhagavan Das, with whom I made acquaintance in Benares in 1914. . . .

Your letter confirms me in the conviction I arrived at during my trip to India, that there is in the world a small number of men united by something, although they may not themselves know it, and may not know one another yet.

> Yours,
> P. OUSPENSKY.

The omitted portions of the letter were devoted to a discussion of ways and means whereby he and his family might be enabled to come to England or America, an enterprise in which he asked our help.

Though we were powerless to be of assistance here,

* Ouspensky made these changes in the second edition and provided an Introduction as well.

[199]

I felt so sure that it was in the pattern of his life to come actively in contact with those English-speaking people who had been spiritually awakened by his book, that I wrote him of my conviction that help would be forthcoming from some person or persons whom he had, in so different a way, himself helped. He could scarcely have received my letter when I received the following telegram from Washington:

Tertium Organum interests me passionately. Desire very much to meet you if possible. Leaving for England end of month.

— VISCOUNTESS ROTHERMERE.

I wired back that I should be glad to see and talk with her, and a few days later she arrived in Rochester.

No sooner did she get from us Ouspensky's address than she cabled him the assurance that she would finance the journey to England, and sponsor him there. This promise was faithfully kept.

The above facts are known by now to quite a large number of people, but one aspect of the whole affair I shall here present for the first time. My wife consulted her oracle, as she called it, about almost everyone and everything that entered our lives in an important way, and after Bessaraboff's first visit she received the following:

" *Eugenie, he is to be ready to follow the call of the voice that is sending an emissary to him. Truly are men being chosen, gathered into groups, and from these groups will come many ties of the spirit to bind the men of one heart into a great brotherhood filled by action of liberation as none others have been."*

Here follow a number of other messages received during the time when we were engaged upon the work of translation, the final two after the reading of the proofs:

" The book is important as it sets forth in language that the uninstructed can understand, the great truth that the future lies with the men who realize the spirit as the potent force by which alone the physical can be completely conquered. Let him proceed with the translation: all difficulties will be cleared for him."

" The book they are doing is one that the Masters of Wisdom have sent to open the minds of men to the new order. The days to come are to see greater changes in the current of life than has been known by the race now living, and a new principle must come into life if the opening of new horizons is to bring knowledge, and not cast into chains the men of the new race."

" The book will be of great assistance to the spreading of the truth necessary to the understanding of us through disciples who will accept our unseen guidance. Let him have no fear, but proceed with high courage."

[201]

" *The book is very necessary to tie in one bond men of the one spirit. It is intended as a precursor: another will follow which could not be understood without the discipline of this.*"

" *The work they have been doing has been accomplished in love. The book is of great and far-reaching importance. Not that it is so remarkable, tried by the wisdom that has been given to man and from which he has blindly turned, but because it offers through a common channel, known to the blind in spirit, a full presentment of truths that men must accept if they are to go forward as sons of the light.*"

" *The work accomplished is our work. It is destined to have a profound influence on many men whose work would be sterile without this new light.*"

I found the writing of the introduction a difficult matter, and often when I was in doubt how to proceed, appealed to the oracle for guidance and light. The following three messages were received in answer to such appeals:

" *He is to speak of the coming time when men will hold their higher selves as the realities, and this that they may know the shell; for in the future men who attain to illumination will treat the lower self as the cast-off sheath, and think of it as an instrument.*"

" *Let him make clear the meaning of superman. He is human, but with dormant faculties alert. Men do not realize the blindness of themselves living in darkness. The illuminated man sees the darkness from the light.*"

" *He has expressed our meaning. It is very necessary that this be told, because men must accept the truth if they are to go forward: unless they recognize in men of high spiritual development leaders, they cannot go forward, but will stay closed in by darkness.*"

When it became necessary to decide how and by whom the book was to be published, and if I were to publish it myself, how it was to be distributed and sold, the oracle had this to offer:

" *He could not do better than to keep the book within his power, for it is to be of infinite power and many will read.*"

" *Let the work take its own course: we will put it in the hands of those whose hearts are open. Only the men who have overpassed the truths of the intellect will understand.*"

" *The work is very great: its importance to men of your mind cannot be described in words. It should go forth lovingly. Too swiftly cannot he accomplish the necessary labor.*"

These quotations will doubtless arouse skepticisms in the minds of many readers which I shall not attempt to allay, and provoke questions in the minds of many which I shall not try to answer. Suffice it to say that we believed the messages and acted in accordance with them, and their prophecies with regard to the importance of the book, and its effect upon the mind of the younger generation, have already proven true. Tertium Organum sold so rapidly that I was obliged to turn it over to Mr. Knopf, under whose imprint it is now in its ninth printing. It has been the subject of spirited controversy and vivid discussion, and its function more and more reveals itself to be as stated — to *tie in one bond men of the one spirit.*

XXIII

THE IMMORTAL RESIDUE

ADELAIDE CRAPSEY died in her thirty-sixth year, on the eighth of October, 1914, of tuberculosis of the throat. Outside of the small circle of relatives and friends who survived her she is known only by a slender volume of posthumous verse, the last testament of a spirit all unreconciled, flashing " unquenched defiance at the stars." This book, with sure prescience, she entitled The Immortal Residue:

> Wouldst thou find my ashes? Look
> In the pages of my book:
> And, as these thy hand doth turn,
> Know here is my funeral urn.

For since her death that urn by the consensus of opinion of all poetry lovers has been given a place in the Poets' Corner of the Westminster Abbey of the mind. Her verse has won highest praise in highest quarters, it is represented in nearly all the new anthologies, certain of her lyrics have been set to music by eminent composers, and she has come to occupy a place among the women poets of America second only to that of Emily

Dickenson, with whose name hers is often coupled, for they are twin stars in the same galaxy.

Adelaide Crapsey was my friend. It was my privilege to edit, introduce and publish her poems, the existence of which were not known until after her death. To realize how tragic that death was, and how greatly resented, it is only necessary to read To the Dead in the Graveyard Underneath My Window, written at Saranac Lake while she was lying, fatally stricken, " with pillow and counterpane for stone and sod." Even so, in the fell grip of " the despot of our days and lord of dust " it was part of her gallantry still to fight on:

> And I will clamor it through weary days
> Keeping the edge of deprivation sharp,
> Nor with the pliant speaking on my lips
> Of resignation, sister to defeat.
> I'll not be patient. I will not lie still.

Like a mother dying with an unborn child, she could not but have been secretly preoccupied with that " immortal residue " of which no one except herself knew anything. Denied survival, she would still live in that only part of herself which had resisted the fire which consumed her: through it, all the world should know " the pacing of her sable-sandalled feet " —

> For the forgotten dead are dead indeed.

After a silence which has lasted fourteen years, I am now going to reveal something which happened after

[206]

Adelaide's death — something quite unsought, surprising and unexpected, for neither my wife — who was concerned in it — nor I are "spiritists" notwithstanding our belief that we are all *projections* upon the lighted screen of this material life of a spirit which is immortal in the sense that it transcends those categories which we call time and space.

It is necessary to remind the reader that my wife was a psychic: a perfectly poised, healthy, beautiful woman, highly cultured and of wide worldly experience, she was gifted with the power to receive from some unknown source, through the instrumentality of automatic writing, communications which cast an illumination upon life, striking the true Delphic note of prophecy, wisdom, rapture. She was not, however, "mediumistic" in the ordinary sense, that is, she never received what purported to be messages from "the dead" except in three instances: every year on the anniversary of his death she received a message from her former (deceased) husband; again, she received the series given in The Black Lacquer Chest, and the third instance related to Adelaide Crapsey. Concerning this I shall now give the facts.

On the eighteenth of July, 1915, on arising she asked me if I knew anybody by the name of Adelaide, for she had been awakened from a medley dream — the incidents of which she failed to remember — by the word "Adelaide! Adelaide!" I suggested that it must have some reference to Adelaide Crapsey or her mother — whose name was the same — and advised her to consult her oracle about it. After the performance of the accustomed ritual, which consisted of the washing of the hands, the preparation of the desk, the burning of incense, the making of the sign of the cross, followed by a few moments of silent meditation with closed eyes, she took up her pen, and in that fine, round back hand, so different from her own running and angular handwriting, received the following message:

" Eugenie, it is an attempt to reach you; she is sad for her mother."

Whereupon I suggested that we both call upon Mrs. Crapsey, which we did that same afternoon, and on our return the following message came, this time in the first person singular, as though from Adelaide herself:

" Know that I am grateful. It is full of terror that I came, but I am glad I doffed the body. Life has been so full here, and I have known things impossible to the flesh. I am going now."

On the following afternoon a conversation about the relation between Adelaide and her mother and the affectional bond between them was the occasion of the following message:

" Great grief purifies and the terror of coming brought
[208]

us together. It is not remorse, but love for her and for him. My father needs faith."

On July the twentieth this came:

" Let me tell you again my story. I died in terror, but I found here a strange new beginning. It was a work full of anguish, but blessed to do. The life that follows death is all so different but so full of thought."

I asked what we could tell her father and mother, and this was the reply:

" You are good to try. I want them to know that I am glad I died, glad I died. I do not want life; this is so rich in experience."

My wife affirmed that as her hand wrote this message she was inundated, so to speak, with a strange gladness, that she felt an unaccountable exultation of spirit, different from anything she had ever known.

Shortly after all this happened, Doctor and Mrs. Crapsey came to me for advice about the publication of Adelaide's verse, which had been found, carefully prepared and arranged, among her effects. They had submitted it to one or two publishers without success. I read the manuscript, sensed its quality, and engaged to publish the book myself, and write the introduction if they so wished. It was during the preparation of this last that my wife received the following message:

" This immortal residue contains the pearl of a heart sick with terrible despair. It has in it all the poignancy and power of a strong, brave soul doing battle with the Silent Watcher. She left another side of her nature, the work on prosody." *

In the writing of the introduction I was naturally desirous of drawing a true and vivid portrait of the author as I knew and remembered her. There was an indefinable moonlit, pearly quality about her; she loved to dress in grey, as she herself has said, in Fate Defied:

> As it
> Were tissue of silver
> I'll wear, O Fate, thy grey,
> And go mistily radiant, clad
> Like the moon.

Apropos of my pen portrait, when it was finished to my satisfaction, the oracle had this to say:

" Let the picture stay: she was a figure of romance, full of the joy and lilt of life. She seemed ever to use the pearl of things unseen; the silence of the deep surrounded her and she came like a wraith to depart again silently into the unseen. The pearl is the symbol of mystery and charm, it personified her well."

The pearl symbol does not appear in my description, for I wanted that to be direct and simple and unencum-

* A fragment of this was afterwards published under the title A Study in English Metrics.

bered with symbol or simile, but nevertheless the *thought* of her pearliness was a controlling factor in that description.

When all difficulties had been at last overcome, and the book was safely and successfully under way, there came this final message.

"*It is well, I am pleased, accept my gratitude. You have done me a great service; I thank you from the country of the free in thought; so good bye, Adelaide Crapsey.*"

I am quite aware that all this is of small evidential value as establishing the survival of the personal consciousness after death, yet from my knowledge of Adelaide's character, the circumstances surrounding her death, and her relation to her parents, the messages seem strangely apposite. Her one desire before she died was to save those she loved most from the pain of her own suffering, despair and frustration. As I said in the introduction to her poems, " Of her passionate revolt against the mandate of her destiny she spared her family and friends even a sign. With a magnificent and appalling courage she gave forth to them the humor and gaiety of her unclouded years, saving them even beyond the end from the knowledge of this beautiful and terrible testament of a spirit all unreconciled." The messages seem to me to have her own strange " soul-color," and this at least is certain: the last unexpressed wish on the near side of the grave — to comfort her parents — was the first to which the oracle gave utterance. Surely, if a liberated spirit such as hers must have been should consent to return to the place of its purgation, would it not be for that?

INDEX OF THE NAMES
OF PERSONS

INDEX

CLAUDE BRAGDON was born in Oberlin, Ohio in 1866. Since then he has been an architect with many notable American buildings to his credit, a philosopher and mystic who has succeeded in elucidating the fourth dimension to an ever growing number of readers, a writer who at first published and still designs his own books and a stage designer from whose hands come all the settings and costumes for the Hampden productions. Out of the experiences of his long and varied career he has produced this book, different in character and attitude from his former work and an expression of the still widening sphere of his many interests.